PRAISE FOR KAREN FINLEY

"In her highly visceral, startling monologues, Ms. Finley forthrightly confronts urgent issues: prejudice, censorship, and most of all, the abuse of women. She is the perfomance artist whose name is synonymous with controversy."
—MEL GUSSOW, *The New York Times*

"At its best, Finley's art rips big, unspoken, and dificult to articulate secrets out of the closet. Her work reminds women that there's no dividend in pleasing and obliging. Being nice hasn't earned women a bloody thing, she says. Her art says that everything, including male privilege, is impermanent. It also says that there are worse things than shit to eat—like eating your heart out when what you really want to do is draw blood."
—LAURIE STONE, *Ms. Magazine*

"Finley is a real artist, who makes art to understand why she makes art. Her central themes are love and pain with riptides of rage."
—PETER SCHJELDAHL, *Village Voice*

A DIFFERENT KIND OF INTIMACY

ALSO BY KAREN FINLEY

Shock Treatment

Enough is Enough

Living it Up

Pooh Unplugged

A DIFFERENT KIND OF INTIMACY

THE COLLECTED WRITINGS OF
KAREN FINLEY

THUNDER'S MOUTH PRESS • NEW YORK

PUBLISHED BY
THUNDER'S MOUTH PRESS
A DIVISION OF AVALON PUBLISHING GROUP INCORPORATED
841 BROADWAY, FOURTH FLOOR
NEW YORK, NY 10003

LIBRARY OF CONGRESS CATALOGING-IN-PUBLICATION DATA

FINLEY, KAREN.
    A DIFFERENT KIND OF INTIMACY : THE COLLECTED WRITINGS OF KAREN FINLEY / BY KAREN FINLEY.
        P. CM.
    ISBN 1-56025-293-6
    I. TITLE.

PS3556. I488 D54 2000
818'.5409—DC21

                                    00-044295

DESIGNED BY PAULINE NEUWIRTH,
NEUWIRTH & ASSOCIATES, INC.

DISTRIBUTED BY PUBLISHERS GROUP WEST

MANUFACTURED IN THE UNITED STATES OF AMERICA

DEDICATION

My women friends have always been a source of great wisdom and strength. My dear friend, the photographer Dona McAdams has been a tremendous support, and Johanna Went, a brillant artist and performer, has been a continued source of inspiration. I dedicate this book to these two women.

ACKNOWLEDGMENTS

A SPECIAL HEARTFELT thanks to Neil Ortenberg for his inspiration and determination.

To all of the Finleys, Joe Steinert, Brian Routh, Jim Grigsby, Dan Geisler, Andy Levis, Victoria Martin and the Imperials, Tony Adler, Tony Labat, Bruce Pollack, Linda Montano, Howard Fried, Kathy Brew, David Ross, John Killacky, Michael Overn, Martha Wilson, Mark Russell, Hudson, Cornelius Conboy, Dennis Gatra, Carlo McCormick, Mark Kamins, Steve Lewis, Tom Murrin, Stuart Cornfield, Scott Macaulay, Ira Silverberg, Bobbi Tsumagari, Cee Brown, Philip Yenawine, Alex Gray, Joy Silverman, David Cole, Mary Dorman, Ellen Yaroshevsky, Marjorie Heins, Ed Degrazia, Holly Hughes, Tim Miller, John Fleck, Timothy Greenfield-Sanders, Ellen Curley, Anne Pasternak, Thomas Healy, Rene Fotouhi, Mike Osterhout, David West, Andy Soma, Carol McDowell, Billy Ehret, Julie Lazar, Tom Finkelspearl, John Stewart, Kim Light, Anne MacDonald, Amy Scholder, Nina Sobel, Emily Hartzell, Jim Simpson, Lori E. Seid, Nancy Gray, Jon Ritter, Rebecca Kamens, Jon Bewley, Simon Hubert, Becky Hubbert, Chris Fleming, Bob Brustein, Rob Orchard, Jed Wheeler, Chris Tanner, Chris Fleming, C. Carr, Lori Stone, Harry Philbrick, Linda Greenberg, Joe Shanahan, Lydia Lunch, Glenn Max, Nick Lawerence, Chris Busa, Ed Cardoni, Tom Borrup, Ann Patty, Virginia Reath, Susan Martin, Tom Patchett, Jim Dobson, Annie Liebovitz, Tom Rauffenbart, Barney Rosset, Astrid Meyers, Annie Philbin, Ellen Salpeter, and Tom Murrin. And to the staff of Thunder's Mouth Press, Dan O'Connor, Ghadah Alrawi, Marie Catheline Jean-Francois, and Matthew Trokenheim.

CONTENTS

Introduction   xiii

1   Sheis Fleis   1

2   Burlesque   9

3   *I'm an Ass Man*   15

4   Unnatural Acts   27

5   Bad Music Videos   31

6   No Entiendes   37

7   *The Constant State Of Desire*   45

8   *A Suggestion Of Madness*   57

9   *The Black Sheep*   67

10   Public Support   77

11   *We Keep Our Victims Ready*   83

12   Politics   99

13   *A Woman's Life Isn't Worth Much*   107

14	A Certain Level of Denial	113
15	Momento Mori	153
16	Enough is Enough	165
17	Living it Up	173
18	Installations	181
19	The American Chestnut	191
20	Uncommon Sense	231
21	Supreme Court	249
22	The Return of the Chocolate-Smeared Woman	253
23	Healing Hollywood Style	265
24	Erotica	273
25	Art World	279
26	Shut Up and Love Me	285
27	Tongues of Flame	309
28	Born to Raise Hell	319

KAREN FINLEY, THE "chocolate-smeared woman" of Jesse Helms's worst nightmares, is a performance artist as provocateur. Specializing in self-exposure, both physical and emotional, she places herself on the firing line and dares her audience to be offended. Yes, she can be outrageous, and readers may be disturbed by the more graphic elements of her book, just as theatergoers have been shocked by aspects of her act. But make no mistake: through her art she exercises a valid political purpose.

Though she often draws her material straight from her life, it is transmogrified into something generic and metaphorical. Her principal subject is Woman, as debased and abused by a male-centered society. As Karen says, we keep our victims ready. As a victim, she has become an accuser, taking a firm stand against those who would censor and limit freedom, and those who act out of prejudice.

For her, performance is catharsis, as it should be for theatergoers watching her. If one is disturbed by her immodesty onstage and in print, it must be remembered that everything is for a reason. Her art is meant to be redemptive, an attempt, in other words, "to lay the moral compass for others to live up to." This is in direct contrast to sensationalists and to those like the Farrelly Brothers who use vulgarity simply for entertainment purposes. Karen is a social activist, and she has her artistic precedents, reaching back beyond the Living Theater to "Ubu" and Artaud.

In the performing arts, her closest kin is Lenny Bruce, who was also a pioneer in freeing speech from self-imposed restrictions, in bringing private matters into the open. Similarly, with Karen, language knows no boundaries. "Unspeakable Practices, Unnatural Acts," that first newspaper headline that brought her to the attention of a wider audience, is a misrepresentation. In defiance of the religious right and others who are sanctimonious, all her practices are speakable, all acts (well, almost all acts) are natural, as long as they are not harmful to health or sanity.

Karen's mother, Mary Finley, who saw all her shows, said, "It took me a while to see what she was trying to do, to show what's going on underneath the garden. I guess the only way you can do that is to rake it up." She was firmly convinced about her daughter's integrity. "I've also seen so much obscenity in my life," she said, "This child of the world is not obscene. One of the things I admire about Karen is that she is open to the world. She just has courage to stick to her belief system, and, I want to tell you, she has the kindest heart."

In her book, Karen reveals aspects about herself, beginning with her family, which for generations has been burdened by dysfunctionalism and depression, for her, culminated when she was 21 with the suicide of her father. When she reads aloud her father's suicide note (reprinted in this book), this may be too intimate for others to bear, as he knowingly abandons his wife and children and himself. In Chapter Eight, she offers a poignant glimpse into the demons of her family background.

There have been other tragedies in Karen's life, including the death of her mother and death of many of her colleagues and friends as a result of AIDS. One of her primary life supports is her sense of humor. There is a comical side to her, as she mocks herself and certainly as she ridicules those who would condemn her, as in her suggested lawsuit against Senator Helms for sexual harassment. She is the scourge of the United States Supreme Court, except, it would seem, for David Souter, the wisest judge of them all, and the only one to cast a vote on her behalf during her long running case.

What was the danger of the NEA four? When one considers the minuscule amount of money they were to receive from the National

Endowment for the Arts, as well as the relatively small size of their collective audience, they can hardly be considered a threat to the Republic. They are alternative voices, to be heard, and to be recognized.

Perhaps the most shocking thing about her is her idealism, which leads her to think, or at least to hope, that she can do all the things she wants to do and not be silenced. She keeps going her own way: writing, performing, undercutting icons, upbraiding hypocrites, baring herself in public (and in *Playboy*) and, when she feels like it, even painting pictures of lush bouquets of flowers. Karen Finley is someone who cannot—and should not—be ignored, as she shows us what's going on underneath the garden.

Mel Gussow is a cultural writer for The New York Times and a critic and author. His most recent book is the biography, Edward Albee: A Singular Journey. He has also written books about Harold Pinter, Tom Stoppard, and Samuel Beckett, and Theatre on the Edge: New Visions, New Voices, a collection of theater reviews and essays.

A DIFFERENT KIND OF INTIMACY

HERE'S NO WAY to put this delicately: I turned around and Brian was lapping up my shit. I was shocked, but the audience seemed to take it in stride. After all, this was West Germany and they had seen it all. The German avant-garde had Hermann Nietzsche, who did performances where he slaughtered animals on church steps, and Gunther Brus, who supposedly cut off his dick during a performance.

1

SHEIS FLEIS

It was 1981, the summer before I received my MFA from the San Francisco Art Institute. Brian and I were touring Europe. In Italy, we had performed in Piazenzia, Rimini, Ravenna, and Bologna. We made our own "spaghetti Western," involving buckets and buckets of spaghetti, and we did pieces on abortion, Mussolini, the Church, and of course, the Pope. While we were in Italy, the Pope was shot, but we didn't stop satirizing him in our performances. The Italians weren't offended—in fact, they loved us for it.

So when Brian and I went on to Cologne for the Theater of the World Festival, we thought the Germans would be equally fun-loving about the performance we had planned—a musical comedy, with the two of us playing Hitler and Eva Braun. We were wrong.

BRIAN ROUTH CAME to the San Francisco Art Institute as a visiting artist in the fall of 1980. He was half of the performance duo The Kipper Kids, a.k.a. Brian Routh and Martin von Haselberg. The Kipper Kids had opened for Led Zeppelin and other bands, so their following extended beyond the boundaries of the art world. They were famous, or infamous. They were these two boy-monsters doing extraordinary work—perverse, singing, wanking, deliciously entertaining vaudevillian art. Martin was German, Brian English. They performed throughout Europe, slathering themselves in paint, having "self-boxing matches" where they punched themselves until they bled, setting off firecrackers hidden in mounds of shaving cream they had placed atop their heads.

I took a class that Brian instructed. I was immediately attracted to him, and soon, he and his white boxer, Harriet, had moved in with me. We began collaborating on performances.

The Theater of the World Festival is a biannual international festival, held in a different German city every year. That year, in Cologne, Laurie Anderson and Pina Bausch were on the bill, along with the seminal performance group Squat Theater and a number of other artists I was interested in.

To prepare for our performance, we went to a butcher shop and got leftover meat, bones, and animal parts that we planned to hang from hooks all over the stage. I bought wursts and sauerkraut, and we also got some beer. All of this was going to be used as props.

HOOLA HOOP
wires w/ sausages
sauercraut
Sourkraut ice cream cones

K saurcraut & susage chest dinner

B Reaper sausage & surkraut
mustard diaper

2

mongoloid Hitler while Karen
covers B w/ lots of food
stuffing in the / mouth

Chop shoulder

hanging Chops

B/ underwear   K/ driving

B/ grinding meat   K/ melons Bratskra
thru audience   pliers weiner
                              feeding

raw meat stuffed or gerkins

goggles

K feed B with chest dinner on plate
(break) plates on head

On the day of our first performance, I came down with a bad case of diarrhea. There were no bathrooms in the circus tent in which Brian and I were going to be doing the show, so I went to the nearby public restrooms. What I didn't know was that, in Germany, to use the public toilets you had to pay four fenningers—approximately four cents. I didn't have any money with me and there was no way I was getting out of the long line to go get some. By the time my turn came, I was frightened that I was literally about to explode, and so I rushed into the toilet without paying. The attendant came in after me, screaming that I was a dirty, filthy American. She began pulling me off the toilet. I told her that I was performing in the festival, but she kept on screaming at me and demanding her goddamn four cents.

I was banned from the public restroom because of the disturbance I'd caused. So I had no choice—I had to make my own toilet. The producers of the festival obligingly provided me with several buckets for this purpose. I put them off stage. But the tent didn't really have a backstage and there was nowhere to put them where they would be completely invisible to the audience.

The performance began smoothly, but a few minutes into it I had to go off stage and use the bucket. Then I came back out and continued with the performance, pretending to eat the wursts and sauerkraut which I had stuffed into my bra. At one point, I turned around and there was Brian, in the character of Hitler, lapping up my shit.

It's widely believed that Hitler couldn't achieve sexual gratification without being pissed on or shit on. Brian, who was drinking very heavily at the time, apparently just couldn't resist this opportunity for a bit of hyper-realism.

The show went on. We got to the dog-impersonation number, where we poured beer into dog bowls, got down on all fours, and drank it, barking and growling like dogs. Suddenly, the audience became agitated. They began screaming at us in English, "The Germans are not dogs!" We ignored them and went on with the act, which also involved smushing chocolate pudding in each other's rear ends and sniffing it til our faces were a brown mess. The sight of Brian lapping up actual shit hadn't bothered the audience, but they became enraged at the sight of Hitler and his mistress portrayed as butt-sniffing dogs. They started yelling that the Germans shouldn't have to see this, that the war was over.

A young woman stepped out of the audience and onto the stage. She picked up a mop and started hitting me on my back, shoulders, and head, screaming, "We Germans are peace-loving people!" Brian picked the woman up and, with a combination of strength and adrenaline, threw her back into the audience. With that, the crowd went wild. They began surging toward the stage. Brian and I took off—running from the stage and out into the street, covered in sauerkraut and chocolate pudding, with about a hundred people chasing us. I really thought we'd be stoned to death once they caught us, but luckily we lost them.

The next day, all of our props were gone and our stage was in total disarray. We met with the festival officials, who told us that they could "no longer guarantee our personal safety." They were extremely unhappy with us, to put it mildly. All they had wanted, they explained, was some "light comedic performance art." This *was* a musical comedy, we told them.

They would have canceled on us, but Fassbinder saved us. The filmmaker had been in the audience the night before and he had loved our show. He was making a documentary of the festival, and he wanted to come back that night and film us. So we were able to perform that night, with Fassbinder filming. The house was packed, and the show was a success. But I've never been invited back to the Theater of the World festival.

*Performing with Brian Routh at the Randolph St. Gallery
in Chicago—1983*

With Laurie (dancer) behind
The Ahole Gallery after
performance—1979

E. M. CURLY

I N 1977, WHEN I took the train out to California to begin my first semester at the San Francisco Art Institute, I met Lowell George, the lead singer of Little Feat. He invited me to come see him perform in San Francisco that night. That was my introduction to the music scene. I started going to the Mabouhey Gardens. I witnessed the emergence of punk—the Mutants, Tuxedo Moon, NOH MERCY, the

2

BURLESQUE

NuNs, the Dils, the Dead Kennedys. I marveled at the performances, the intensity of the movement.

People in San Francisco at that time still remembered the summer of love, the riots, the anti-war demonstrations, Patty Hearst, SDS, the black panthers.

There was a lot of radical creativity going on. Mark Pauline of Survival Research Laboratories made huge war machines with a sense of both irony and spectacle. The music scene was creating clubs out of nowhere; they were all over the city. The most unusual was probably The Deaf Club—an actual club for the deaf, where you would see deaf people feeling the walls for vibrations from the intense punk music.

When I first got to San Francisco I worked odd jobs, scooping ice cream, hostessing at the Top of the Mark. Then I found the money. I began working at The Condor Club in North Beach.

The Condor was the first topless club in America. Carol Doda was the premier act—there was a giant neon sign in her image, with boobs that flashed on and off. Other Art Institute girls worked there. I was a waitress, along with my girlfriend Ellen. We weren't topless, but we were cocktail waitresses, asking for service fees with every drink we served.

None of the women had fake breasts or nose jobs or liposuction. (Except Carol Doda. Hers were the first silicone breasts, and they were *huge.*) I remember the barker talking about how different all the women were—that was one of the attractions. The Condor featured big butts and little ones, sagging breasts and perky ones. The women didn't dwell

Performing with Bruce Pollack at the Mabouhey Gardnes   E.M. CURLEY

on their imperfections. They'd focus on what they had—great legs, a tiny waist or a long neck. These were women who knew burlesque. Some were pushing 50, but they'd come out on stage in blue velvet and just show an ankle and the room would be wet.

IN 1978, WHILE I was in my hometown of Chicago for Christmas break, my father committed suicide. I felt a tremendous sense of numbness, shock, and despair, and the only thing that got me through it was thinking about how I had lost everything, and there wasn't anything more to lose.

I started making more intense, emotional work. I consciously made the decision to turn my disadvantages to my advantage. I made use of the fact that I was a woman, of my "hysteria," and my body.

I had my first run-in with the law. I'd been doing a performance as part of a series curated by my friend and fellow artist Mike Osterhout. The performances were done in the window of an abandoned JC Penney in downtown San Francisco. I appeared via motorcycle—I rode right into the building and into the window. Then I smashed several dozen overripe bananas into my mouth, and started smooshing my body up against the window, slobbering and kissing it in a mix of red-light-district prostitute and locked-up psychopath. A crowd gathered that blocked the sidewalk and spread into the street. The police showed up, and my performance was stopped. I was put into a squad car (though Mike Osterhout talked the police out of arresting me). The strange thing was that the police kept saying, "This woman is nude, insane, and on drugs." Apparently the person who had called the police had described me that way, and the police were repeating the description, even though they could see that I was fully clothed. It was like "The Emperor's New Clothes" in reverse.

That was the end of the performance series at JC Penney—and the beginning of my career causing psychic disturbances.

Performing at Franklin Furnace

AFTER THE EUROPEAN TOUR, Brian and I decided to get out of San Francisco. We moved to Chicago, the city where I had grown up. Back then, Chicago was what L.A. is today—the American art world's second city. *Artforum* reviewed Chicago shows in every issue. There was an active and vibrant art scene happening.

3

I'M AN ASS MAN

In 1983, Brian and I were invited to do a show at Franklin Furnace in New York City on a double bill. I did a performance where I took a bath in a suitcase and shoveled milk off the floor, and Brian did one of his own pieces. Sally Banes gave us a great review in the *Village Voice*.

Brian and I started thinking about moving to New York, but it was hard to save the money we would need. I was a waitress at a restaurant in a luxury hotel. Brian was teaching at the Chicago Art Institute and working as a doorman on top of that.

I had applied to the National Endowment for the Arts, and, in October of 1983, they awarded me a grant of five thousand dollars. That was more money than I had ever had. I put it all in a cash belt and I went to New York to find an apartment for Brian and I.

I found a sublet in the East Village, which most people still considered an undesirable place to live. It was a decent building on a street filled with Ukrainian dairies, Jewish delis, and drug dealers. Within a couple of years, I'd be seeing my friends buying heroin on my block.

The East Village at that time had a self-contained art world, complete with its own paper, the *East Village Eye*. It had two galleries: Civilian Warfare and Gracie Mansion. It had a few clubs: the Pyramid; 8BC, which was an old farmhouse with a huge stage in the basement; and Limbo, a storefront club. These were the places where everything happened—the performances, the parties, the openings.

I started performing at downtown spaces, where, as usual, I was paid virtually nothing. But the exhilaration wasn't about making money, or even being discovered—it was about creating a scene, an identity.

I made a living by waiting tables at Cafe Central, a chic uptown restaurant. Bruce Willis was a bartender there at the time. I waited on Cher and Robin Williams. Soon, though, I got a job waiting on cooler celebrities. I became a cocktail waitress at a new club, Area.

Area was below SoHo, in TriBeCa. To this day it remains the most extraordinary club I have ever been to. The owners were like

Performing at Area

conceptual artists with a brilliant and unique vision. Area had a dance floor, a separate lounge with an aquarium and a fish pond, and a VIP lounge. Throughout the club, there were store windows with installations or tableaux created by local artists. Slides, films and videos were projected onto the walls, and paintings and sculpture were on display. The club had a different theme every month, and the decor, the art, everything, was always changing according to the theme.

Area instantly became the trendiest place to see and be seen. I worked in the VIP lounge. I got to know the owners and managers, and started curating the "Obsession" nights for the summer of 1984. My co-curators (Howard Schaeffer, the manager, and publicist Joe Dolce) and I picked a different obsession every week—food, sex, drugs, religion. We would commission performances based on the obsession. For our "Religion" night, Linda Montano, who did brilliant time-based performances, heard confessions in the bathroom. Andy Soma did a piece where he impersonated a drug kingpin, cutting lines of fake coke as long as the bar (some people thought they were real). We showed the extraordinary artist Carolee Schneeman's erotic film *Fuse*. Brian performed, naked, painted all white with one brown eye, sniffing and crawling around on all fours.

In the fall of 1984, I left Area to become a bartender at Danceteria. Danceteria was four floors of pure club entertainment, plus a roof that was open in the summertime. The crowd was younger and more cutting-edge than the one at Area. At Area, there was a kind of Fifth Avenue couture vibe, while at Danceteria people were more into the S&M look—corsets, spikes, leather. There was more variety, and more piercing, more drag queens, more drugs, more live music and performance. The cops would come around once in a while but they never really bothered us, even during S&M parties where people's genitalia was exposed. This was the pre-Giuliani era, and partying in New York City was still looked at as an acceptable pastime.

I was hired by Haoui Montaug. Haoui was one of those club-scene personalities who, though he may have been anonymous to most of the world, was famous on the closed circuit of the club scene. He worked at the Palladium after he left Danceteria and was a downtown fixture for many years. Haoui and the DJ Anita Sarko had a monthly showcase, or cabaret, called No Entiendes (which means "You don't understand"). All the downtown acts performed in No Entiendes— John Sex, Ann Magnuson, hip hop acts, the Beastie Boys and Madonna when they were just starting out. Rick Ruben, of Def Jam, hung out listening to the DJs and the new sounds.

I began writing and performing monologues for the cabaret. I used all my anger and intensity in my performances, so that the bombed clubgoers would have to give me their attention. Haoui was impressed. I became a regular performer at Danceteria. Many of the monologues that I performed there came together into a longer piece called *I'm an Ass Man*.

I'M AN ASS MAN

EVEN THOUGH I'M MARRIED and I've got the work and the kids, I can't stop looking at butt. I can't stop looking at derriere. I can't stop looking at tush. And once I spotted her in the subway—short, Hispanic, Polish, Chinese, or Jewish, with a huge big butt just waiting to be fucked, just asking to be fucked. . . . She was short-waisted, and all I wanted to do was get her against the cold, slimy, rat-turd wall. And she is wearing polyester pants, and I can see her underpants line through her pants, she's so fat that the cellulite bunches between her thighs as she walks, I can hear the sound of her fat thighs, swishing as she moves. And she's wearing those 4-inch cork wedges that went out of style in the early seventies.

I wanted to get myself inside her. But first I wanted to feel some of that butt action. That cheek action. Feel some of that butt pressure. All I want to do is get my mitts against the small of her back. I crack open the seat of her pants, just listening to the fabric tear. I love the sound of ripping polyester. Then I get my fist, my hand and I push myself up into her ass. I'm feeling her up. I'm feeling the butt pressure on my arm, on my wrist, it's feeling good. It's turning me on. It's turning me on. I can hear that sound. I'm feeling her up. I reach up to her pussy, feeling that fat little mound, that little birds nest. When I take my hand out I see my arm, my hand, and I see that THE WOMAN HAS HER PERIOD. How could you do this to me, woman? How could you do this to ME! BE THE BEST FUCK IN YOUR LIFE! BE THE BEST PIECE OF COCK IN YOUR LIFE, GIRL! BE THE BEST RAPE IN YOUR LIFE!

And I was running. I'm running, I'm trying to get those purple hearts off of my hands, out of my cuticles, but the blood won't come out of my lifeline, out my heartline, the blood won't wash off of my hands. Be a long time before I use that hand to shake my dick after I piss.

Performing "Mr. Hirsch."

MR. HIRSCH

I WAS SO HAPPY when the Hirsches moved next door. They had a daughter my age and soon I was participating in all their family activities—camping, canoeing, swimming, fishing, baseball. And once I spent the night there. I was washing my hands in the middle of the night after I awoke to pee. Mr. Hirsch came into the bathroom while I was in there. He was wearing his pajamas and his poker was sticking straight out of his bottoms.

And I asked Mr. Hirsch, "What's wrong, Mr. Hirsch?"

And he said, "Oh, I don't feel well. My pee is stuck in my wiener. I'd wake up Mrs. Hirsch or my daughter but their mouths are weak with sleep. And I need my pee sucked out of my penis now or it's going to backtrack into me and I'm going to die."

I said, "My own daddy never had me do this. Can't I call my daddy and ask if I should do this?"

"No, there isn't time. There isn't time," he said. "You don't want me to die, do you? You don't want to be responsible for my death, do you?"

I didn't trust Mr. Hirsch, but I still didn't want him to die. I also didn't want to go to jail.

"All right, Mr. Hirsch, I'll suck your penis for you. But first, you have to stop calling me 'Yo.' And you've got to take those gold chains, that peace sign, and license plate that says 'Sylvester Moses' off your hairy chest, and you got to drop that ghetto blaster too."

So my head slammed tight against the toilet bowl and I'm smelling the cat pan. Get that cat pan away from me! Get that cat pan away from me! I'm smelling last month's flu and Mrs. Hirsch's dropped perfume. Get it away from me. Get it away from me! But no one can hear me because my throat is full of him. And he's saying, "Pretend it's an ice cream cone, pretend it's an ice cream cone."

I can't breathe. My throat hurts. I'm going to die for sure. Stop! Stop! Then I found out that boys' pee tastes different from girls' pee. Boys' pee tastes different from girls' pee.

* * *

Almost all of my income during this time went right to student loans and rent, and my food came from a food kitchen. I didn't have money to spend on props, so I used what I could find. When I was going to be doing a show, I would hit the food kitchen, or I would open up my refrigerator and see what was inside. That's how I started using food in my work. Food provided a primitive, visceral, almost gruesome element. It helped to convey to the audience the ways in which the characters I portrayed were being violated.

The monologues in *I'm an Ass Man* all center on sexual abuse and violence. The title piece is narrated in the voice of a man who's about to rape a woman on the subway. Just as he's about to rape her, he discovers she is menstruating. To illustrate this during my performances, I would open a can of kidney beans into my hands. In "Mr. Hirsch," where the little girl is forced to perform oral sex on her neighbor, I used melted ice cream sandwiches that smash and pop through their wrappers onto the girl's dark dress, to symbolize the neighbor's climax. In "Yams Up My Granny's Ass," a drug addict abuses his grandmother on Thanksgiving:

> . . . So when things get real bad—real bad—I take a can of yams and I stick it up my granny's ass. She's such a fine granny to humiliate, she's such a fine granny to torture, because she's a mute granny. Doesn't make a sound. Her eyes stick out like blue raisins on a rabbit, some furry little animal. I'm smearing her all over with the candied, sugared yams. And I turn her over on her back so the candied syrup sugar yam juice runs down her back, along her spine.
>
> Then I put her under a heat lamp and I let the yam syrup sizzle on her spine—it boils real nice. She's such a nice granny to torture. She's so fine to do it to. Then I put a tab of ecstasy in her cup of Nescafe every morning, and she just looks out and hallucinates all over me . . .

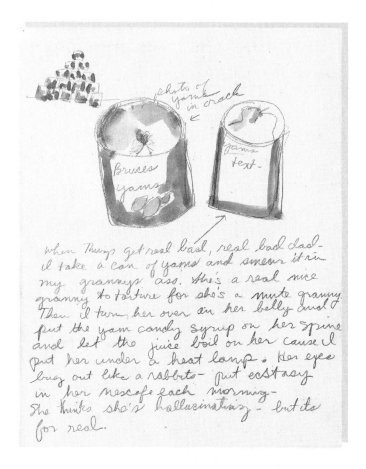

I'd illustrate this by turning my back on the audience, bending down, pulling my dress up, and emptying a can of sugared cooked yams onto my backside, then smearing them on the cheeks and crack of my ass. It was supposed to be a moment of black comedy and that was how my audiences usually took it.

The *Village Voice*'s C. Carr had been following my career for a while. She had a column called "Edge" in which she wrote about me several times. I appeared on the cover of the January 1, 1986 issue of the *Voice* (along with Spike Lee) as "someone to watch" for 1986.

Then C. Carr decided to write a cover story on me and my work in the *Village Voice*. The story—"Unspeakable Practices, Unnatural Acts"—came out in June 1986, and my life changed overnight.

yams

UP MY GRANNY'S ASS

KAREN FINLEY
AT
R.S.G.

FRIDAY APRIL 11 , SATURDAY APRIL 12
5$ GENERAL   4$ STUDENTS/MEMBERS
8:00 PERFORMANCE
RANDOLPH STREET GALLERY
756 N. MILWAUKEE AVE. 666-7737

141133 © VV PUBLISHING CORPORATION

DRAMA CRITICS, R.I.P. (BERMAN, P.28)

Jailhouse Rock

Pete Hamill (P.10)
and Greg Tate (P.63) at
the Amnesty Concert

PLUS

Nat Hentoff
on Mexico's Record
of Abuse (P.25)

the village VOICE

VOL. XXXI NO. 25 • THE WEEKLY NEWSPAPER OF NEW YORK • JUNE 24, 1986 • $1.00

JAMES HAMILTON

UNSPEAKABLE PRACTICES UNNATURAL ACTS

The Taboo Art of Karen Finley

BY C.CARR (P. 17)

Contra-dictions

James Ridgeway on
Reagan's Dirty Little
War (P. 26)

PLUS

Geoffrey Stokes
on PBS's Dirty Little
Movie (P. 8)

TENOR MADNESS

from
Coleman Hawkins
to
Sonny Rollins

A JAZZ SUPPLEMENT

RAYMOND ROSS

THE WEEK AFTER C. Carr's cover story came out, the *Voice* writer Pete Hamill wrote a response piece. Hamill had impeccable liberal credentials. He wrote the liner notes for *Blonde on Blonde,* had dated Jackie O, and had been a big proponent of First Amendment rights.

Hamill's piece was scornful and sarcastic. He condemned C. Carr for choosing to

4

UNNATURAL ACTS

write about me, and he said that my work was "basically worthless." Hamill apparently never went to see the performance that he devoted so many words to excoriating, because he imagined that I actually took an uncooked yam and sodomized myself with it on stage. The article presented me in an entirely sexualized way and didn't even entertain the possibility that I might be talented. It concluded by suggesting that readers send yams to *Voice* editor Robert Friedman, who "would know what to do with it."

I was surprised that I was being attacked not from the right, but from the left. I couldn't understand what it was about the piece that had gotten this liberal guy going. But I realized that it probably had more to do with the state of things at the *Village Voice* than it had to do with me. In 1986, the *Voice* was in a state of flux. The predominately male old guard was being infiltrated by female writers and editors, such as Carr and her editor, Karen Durbin. And the paper was devoting a lot more space to queer issues, which was still not at all a mainstream subject.

To me, Hamill's piece was clearly about the fact that he felt threatened on all fronts. In his article, he displayed an absolute fixation on the idea of the yam in the butthole. His disgust at this idea—and his need to publicly announce his disgust—seemed like an obvious case of homophobic hysteria.

Hamill's piece was a lesson to me. Up until then, I had seen the culture as being divided into liberals vs. conservatives, and I had expected that issues like sexism and homophobia and free speech would always break down along those lines. But now I saw that, more often, they broke down along lines of power.

The pro-yam/anti-yam battle went on for a few weeks. I thought about writing a letter to the *Voice*, but every time I sat down to write, "I never put a yam in my butt," I'd think—but what if I had? SO WHAT? I felt that defending, explaining, clarifying, would somehow be giving in to them. In retrospect, I wish I had had a sense of humor about it, that I had used humor to puncture Hamill's posturing. But

I had so much invested in being taken seriously. I felt that women were always laughed at or sexualized when somebody wanted to shut them up, and I didn't want to risk that happening to me.

I did react to the attacks in one way—they pissed me off so much that I became even more determined to continue doing outrageous work using my body. There was the peaches-in-the-pussy routine, where I put quartered cling peaches beside my labia, and the champagne douche, which is probably self-explanatory.

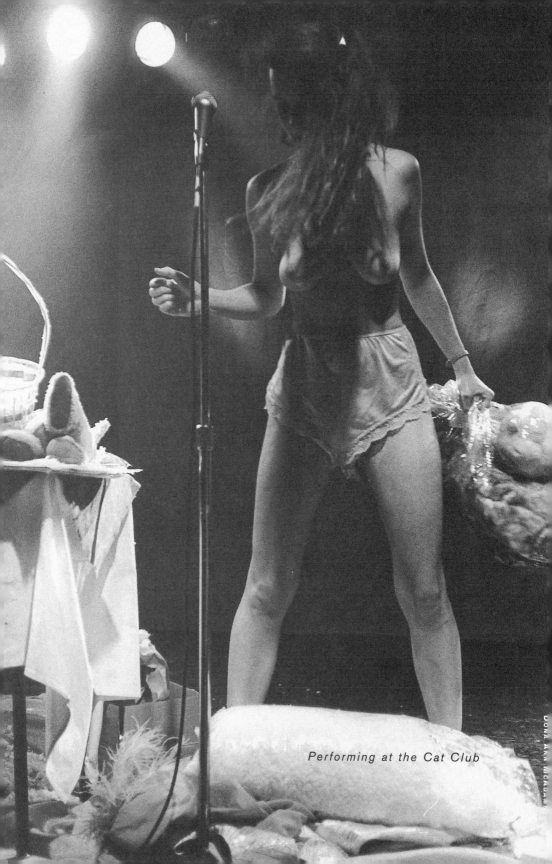

Performing at the Cat Club

CARLO MCCORMICK AND I
were co-hosting a show
called Bad Music Videos,
which we taped in downtown clubs and
broadcast on cable. Carlo was the art critic
for the *East Village Eye* and he also worked
at 8 B.C. He was very striking, with his long
red hair, and was one of the people who
defined the East Village scene. He and I

5

BAD MUSIC
VIDEOS

with Michael Overn shared the same taste for awful, mainstream pop culture, and so we came up with the idea for Bad Music Videos. We'd show music videos and do commentary on them as they played. The videos were hilarious and sometimes macabre: Karen Carpenter; Philip Michael Thomas; Cher; Pia Zadora; Jermaine Jackson; all of them wandering through weird early-MTV landscapes, with girls in bikinis and cheap special effects and fog billowing everywhere. There was so much fog that Carlo and I decided to do a "Night of Fog" at the Cat Club—a night of live performances, but we had a fog machine going the whole time so that the bands looked like they were playing in the middle of a cheesy Bryan Adams video.

Brian and I had broken up in 1985, and I was seeing Michael Overn, who did the videotaping at Danceteria. He was a producer with his own recording studio. The first time I went to Michael's studio, Lydia Lunch was there, remixing *Stinkfist*, a collaboration she did with Jim Foetus. Lydia was making inroads in the male-dominated music industry, not just in terms of the business end of things, but aesthetically. She was a female performer who was aggressive and sexual and angry and brooding, who appropriated aspects of the male rock and roll persona that had been denied to women in the past, or that women had denied themselves. It struck me that there were some parallels between what she was doing in her work and what I did in mine. I became interested in pop music's potential as a medium that I could use in my work.

I had just recorded "I'm an Ass Man" on a record called *The Uproar Tapes*, which featured downtown performers—Eric Bogosian, Ann Magnuson, Ethel Eichelberger. Island, we were told, was scared of it. Mark Kamins, who produced "Lucky Star" for Madonna, was a DJ at Danceteria. He heard my performances and said he wanted to do a dance song with me.

So, in late 1986, I recorded a track for Mark called "Tales of Taboo," with me speaking over Robert Goral's music. The song instantly hit the dance tracks. I recorded more songs—"Lick It," "Sushi Party"—and an album, *The Truth Is Hard To Swallow*. I recorded a remix of Sinead O'Connor's "Jump In The River," and I was sampled on the recordings of other artists, like S Express.

Performing in NEOFEST/April 1983

SUSHI PARTY

THE FIRST THING I'm going to do this year is raise the price of blow jobs. Lying on your back with your legs apart, that's no work at all. But if you want me to swallow your cum, that'll be an extra fin.

This year we broads, bitches, dames, and chicks are going to have the New Year's Eve Party. Boys, we decided we are going to have the party at our house, down by Kenosha, down by Oshkosh, down by Schaumburg, down by Niles, we'll have our party. We get our big glass punch bowl, that big glass bowl like crystal, like plastic. I get myself a bottle of gin, bottle of crème de men-the—make it green—Grand Marnier, crème de cocoa, Jack Daniels—and I put Wild Turkey in that punch bowl. Put the white wine, the chablis, Sprite, over the ice cream that I get from 31 Flavors to give it some head. Like licorice whip, macadamia, chocolate macaroon flavor. Then I clean out the medicine cabinet and I put in Tylenol, aspirin, ampicillin too. (I don't ever put penicillin. Someone might be allergic.) I also take some wart creme and some Hawaiian sensomil-la, and I make a paste with some maraschino juice and put it on the rim of the glasses, like salted margarita glasses. I've got my diarrhea pills, I've got my codeine, my ups and downs. I put all of those pills in the punch and then baby, me and my girls, we get the ecstasy, the dust, and the acid, about 100 tabs. I clean out the entire medicine cabinet and put everything in my party juice.

Then I go over to the cops', because some of us girls's tricks are cops. Cops get the best drugs, cops get the best dust and smoke. Let our gums soak up our dusted, rimmed glasses of blow and cool juice. The cops come to our house for the party, for we give the best party, and we give them some glasses of punch, lots of glasses, until they are puking all over the place—all over the place.

The men are upchucking all over the place, and then it's time for our annu-al sushi party. Well, I open up a can of tuna and I put it into the folds of my vulva, then I stand in front of the men, over the men, and then I say to the men, "SUSHI PARTY BOYS! EAT UP!" They are all out of their minds from the pills and the puking, and they are chewing me, chewing me. Then they say, "This isn't like usual tuna, it's kinda juicy and soggy." Sushi, sushi, juicy sushi. And they are eating me up. I've got my party going. Then the next thing they are doing is, they are pooping all over the place, throwing up all over the place—they've lost control. I don't care, because I have Hefty trashbags all over the place, taped all over the carpet. Mildred doesn't care, she's got her Electrolux to clean it up, but I say, "Wait til tomorrow, Mildred, it peels up like Elmer's Glue." She's my best friend and we girls know how to have a party, so she takes out the Electrolux. Fred sees her with the vacuum and that turns him on. He wants to take that long long tube and work her oyster over. Just work her over. Turn it on baby. Turn it off. Whatever gets you going.

We are all laughing, laughing, and then it's my favorite part of our party, I go and sit over the boys' faces and fart. Fart. 'Cause these men have been farting and passing gas every night. They go and have dinner and they pass gas, they get out of the dinner and they fart, they watchin' their sports and they FART. I keep farting on them until they say, "Please, please don't fart on me. I promise I won't fart and watch sports anymore!"

And then we go and wake up the kids, cause we always abuse our kids. We have intercourse, play with them, and abuse them like hell, man. But tonight we let our kids go free, let them do whatever they want to do with us—firecrackers up our butthole, yeah—ride us like ponies.

* * *

I WROTE SONGS with sexually explicit lyrics in which the woman was on top. I intentionally used a lot of profanity, because I was trying to make a point about the way in which corporate radio stations censored music that contained "bad words." I wasn't interested in being a rock star—I looked at my involvement with music as an art piece. I wanted to appropriate music as a mode of self-expression, and use it to reach out to contemporary culture with real immediacy.

WHEN I GOT off the plane at Heathrow, I knew there was some kind of trouble, because nobody from the Institute of Contemporary Art was there to meet us. It was November, 1986, and I had gone to England to join Haoui Montaug, Anita Sarko, and other No Entiendes performers

NO ENTIENDES

6

for a showcase at the London ICA. I was with Michael and another performer, David Cale.

The three of us made our way to the museum by ourselves. The director, Bill McAllistar, greeted us and led us to the cafeteria. Over tea, McAllistar told us that Scotland Yard was going to be present at my performance that night. In fact, McAllistar went on, there were Scotland Yard agents in the cafeteria at that very moment. We looked around, and sure enough, there were two men in beige raincoats staring at us.

I was planning on doing 7 to 10 minutes of *I'm An Ass Man* for my part of the showcase. I wasn't planning any nudity. Which was a good thing, because in England, they have a law that says a woman can't talk and take off her clothes at the same time. It sounds like the premise of a Monty Python sketch but it's true. Apparently, McAllistar explained, Scotland Yard was there to make sure I didn't start talking and stripping right then and there.

The *Village Voice* articles had circulated internationally, and I had started getting offers to perform abroad. I'd gone to Europe in September 1986 to perform at the Lantaren theater in Rotterdam. *Time Out London* had sent a writer, Alix Sharkey, to Rotterdam, to interview me and write a story about my performance.

Sharkey's article appeared as the cover story in *Time Out* the week of the showcase at ICA. In the article, Sharkey described me as the "high priestess of pornography" and gave a graphic blow-by-blow of my Rotterdam performance, where a woman had gotten offended by me and had come onstage and overturned my table of props. For the cover, the magazine used a photo of me that had originally been used in the *SoHo Weekly*'s Thanksgiving issue. It was a somewhat clumsy and ordinary photo in which I posed in sexy underwear, holding a turkey.

The London *Daily Mail* had picked up on the *Time Out* story, and had contacted Scotland Yard's Clubs and Vice Unit about it, and was generally stirring up a tempest in a teapot about the outrageous antics

Time Out

LONDON'S WEEKLY GUIDE   NOVEMBER 5-12 1986   No.846   80p

UNNATURAL PRACTICES
Karen Finley and the Cabaret of Outrage

EIGHT

MARK JENKINSON
REPRINTED BY PERMISSION
OF TIME OUT

of the "high priestess of pornography"—a phrase I was going to be seeing in several British tabloids over the next few days.

Not only that, but the photo of me on the cover of *Time Out* had caused an outcry with the Brits, who apparently take their birds seriously. Somehow it was construed as being an image of the prelude to some kind of exploitative sexual encounter between me and the turkey. One outraged man wrote to *Time Out* that I was "causing the turkey unnecessary distress."

There was more. A woman named Mary Whitehouse, who had been crusading against "obscenity" in Britain for some time, had turned her attention to me. If you can imagine Tipper Gore and Anita Bryant rolled into one, with a British accent, you'll have a good picture of Mary Whitehouse. One of Whitehouse's favorite tactics was to have people prosecuted for violations of arcane laws that no one had enforced in decades. Whitehouse had decided that I was guilty of "promotion of buggery." (And, I might add, I was happy to promote buggery.) Moreover, Whitehouse pointed out that, because the ICA was only a few hundred yards from Buckingham Palace, if I performed I would be breaking some ancient law that prohibited "committing indecent acts in proximity to the Queen."

If I performed, I was told, I would very likely be arrested and deported. Not only that, but the ICA might face prosecution. I was outraged by the fact that Britain's major newspapers publish photos of half-naked women every day, but here was everyone saying that it was illegal for me to take off my clothes in the course of an art piece. In other words, if a woman was passive and showed her naked body for the pleasure of men, that was OK. But if she took control of her own nudity, used it to expose abuse and exploitation, then she was subject to arrest.

All the British tabloids had picked up the story, and wherever I went there were photographers surrounding me. The articles that they wrote were preposterous. They nicknamed me "Fruity Karen," said I comitted bestiality, and seemed to be trying to top one another in coming up with vile things I supposedly did during my performances. Someone identified only as "Lady Porter" was quoted in several papers calling my work "absolute rubbish." But the most ridiculous thing of all were the pictures. They superimposed my head on a photo of some other woman's naked body.

The ICA staff urged me to go on British television to "show everyone what a nice young lady" I was, but I felt that that was beside the point. Even if I was a mean old lady, a walking public relations disaster, I should still have been allowed to do my art in peace. I did consent to do a press conference, but I put a bag on my head and turned my back to the reporters. I have to say that, as with the *Voice* controversy, I had no sense of humor about the whole thing. I felt that the political situation I was in was too serious for me to allow myself to be funny or sexy. I was Joan of Arc, a stoic warrior for justice. That was how I was starting to see myself.

Haoui wanted me to risk arrest, to make a statement explaining the work and then perform it. But the political climate in Britain at the time was such that they were looking for someone to make an example of, and I didn't see any reason why I should play into their hands and become that example. I didn't want to be the ICA's martyr or Mary Whitehouse's publicity pawn. And I definitely didn't want to be arrested in a foreign country where there was no First Amendment, no ACLU to protect me. Michael and I decided that it would be best to leave the country. I got the next flight out. Instead of performing in the cabaret, I had a recording of "I'm an Ass Man" played on the sound system while the (standing-room only) audience looked at an empty stage.

The groundbreaking performance artist John Sex was in the showcase. In order to protest what was going on, he did a deliberately "obscene" performance: he performed oral sex on an audience member, danced with a four-foot cardboard penis, and sang pornographic disco songs. John could have been just as much of a publicity bonanza

NO ENTIEN

VINI VIDI

The No Entiendes performers. John Sex is in the center with blonde spiked hair.

A DIFFERENT KIND OF INTIMACY

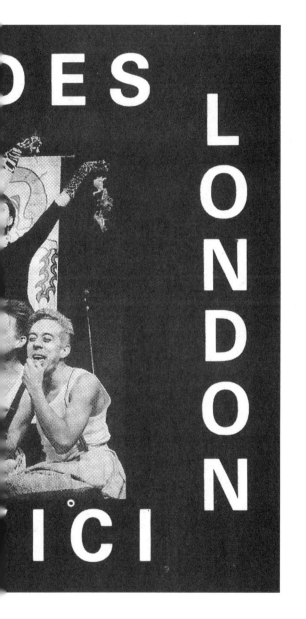

for the tabloids as I was. An onstage blowjob followed by a rendition of "Hustle with My Muscle" certainly seemed to qualify as an "indecent" performance. But nobody arrested John, or even bothered him.

I didn't perform in London for another ten years. By that time, Margaret Thatcher was out of office.

Live Green Room
Manchester

$\mathcal{I}$N THE FALL of 1986, the curator Scott Mcaulay asked me to perform for four nights at the Kitchen. To me, this was the culmination of a fantasy. I had read about the Kitchen in *Artforum* and other magazines as a teenager. It always seemed that the Kitchen was the most exciting place to see and make art.

7

THE CONSTANT STATE OF DESIRE

I didn't rehearse *The Constant State of Desire*. I did the performance spontaneously, and it varied from night to night, in the tradition of performance art. But I was working from a memorized script, in the manner of traditional drama. Performing *The Constant State of Desire* at the Kitchen was a breakthrough for me, in terms of my finding a place between the fine art and theater worlds.

DONNA ANN McADAMS

STRANGLING BABY BIRDS

SHE DREAMS OF strangling baby birds. Bluebirds, wrens, and robins. And with her thumbs she pushes back on their small feathered necks, pushes back against their beaks, till they snap like a breaking twig.

She dreams. She dreams of being locked in a cage and singing loudly and off-key, with her loved ones standing behind her, whispering, "She has an ugly voice. Doesn't she? She has an ugly voice." Oh, leave it to the loved ones to always interfere with our dreams.

She dreams. She dreams of falling out of a fifth-story window. But she catches her fall by holding onto the window ledge. It's January and the ledge is made of stone. The ledge is icy, frozen, and cold. The stone and the ice cut through her flesh, cut through her fingers, her bone. It doesn't matter, though, for she had ugly fingers. And she sees the blood gush out of her limbs the more she holds on to the ledge. She can hear her own death. As she hangs out of the window, her husband walks below. But her husband hasn't memorized her shadow, and she doesn't know how to wear perfume. She just isn't that kind of a girl. So she cries out for help. Help. HELP. Help. HELP! But the wind is in a mean mood and takes her cries halfway round the world, to a child's crib, so its mother can hear her own child's cries.

This dream was considered very important to the doctors. For in the past, she'd had dreams of tortures, rapes, and beatings where no sounds would come out at all. She'd open up her mouth and move her lips, but no sounds would come out at all. You know those dreams. You know those dreams.

But she knew that these doctors were wrong. For these were the same doctors who anesthetized her during the birth of her children. These were the same doctors who called her "animal" as she nursed. These were the same doctors who gave her episiotomies. No more sexual feelings for her during or after childbirth.

But she knew that it really wasn't the doctors' fault. That the problem was in the way she projected her femininity. And if she wasn't passive, well—she just didn't feel desirable. And if she wasn't desirable, she just didn't feel female. And if she wasn't female, well, the whole world would cave in.

Like when my father finally told me he loved me, after 40 years, then went into the bathroom, locked the door, put up pictures of children from the Sears catalogue, arranged mirrors, black stockings and garters to look at as he masturbated while he hung himself from the shower stall. Whatever turns you on, girl. Whatever, whatever turns you on.

And when that man died—volcanoes erupted, cyclones appeared, coyotes came out of their caves, old people were struck by lightning. Don't you know that I don't want any more death on my conscience? I already have an abortion on my conscience from when a member of my own family raped me. Don't worry, I won't mention your name. Don't worry, I won't mention your name. And I know now that the reason my father committed suicide is, he no longer found me attractive.

And by now you can tell that I prefer talking about the fear of living to talking about the fear of dying.

DONA ANN MCADAMS

THE FATHER IN ALL OF US

MY FIRST SEXUAL EXPERIENCE

My first sexual experience was at the time of my birth, passing through the vaginal canal. That red pulsing tunnel, that alley of love. It's the smell of my mama. I'm nothing but a human penis. At the time of my birth, I had an erection. I'm fucking my own mama at birth. It's the smell, it's the sight of my own mama that keeps me going.

So I spend my adulthood driving around in my red car, the symbol of my masculinity, looking for hot mamas with hot titties in hot laundromats, dressed in gingham, the symbol of their martyrdom. I love to find a hot young mama with a bald-headed baby. A brunette, a page boy. I love the smell of the dryer, the sound of the spin cycle, the sight of a woman working a machine. It really turns me on. Oh, gets me going, seeing a woman's body vibrate against a machine. I just take that mama and push her against that washer—then I take her baby, a bald-headed baby, put Downy fabric softener on baby's head—strap that baby around my waist til it's a baby dildo. Then I take that baby, that baby dildo, and fuck its own mama—

CAUSE I'M NOTHING BUT A MOTHER FUCKER! I'M NOTHING BUT A MOTHER FUCKER! Just putting the baby back where it wants to go—back to it's old room, the womb.

Then I reach out for those titties to see if the bitch is still nursing. But she's nothing but a dried old sow. She's nothing but a dried old sow. Then I black out.

And it's twenty years later.

And I'm in my mama's house.

And my mama is still watching the stories. Ma is sprawled out on the avocado-green shag carpeting, wearing her washed-out plaid housecoat. And my mama is still watching all the stories on the TV.

And she smokes her Pall Malls, she smokes her Camels—FLICK THAT ASH MAMA! FLICK THAT ASH! Look at me! Look at me! You never look at me! I'm back, mama. You never looked at me. No, you didn't. I'm nothing to you. So I'll roll my mama's belly onto the shag carpeting. She still not looking at me as I roll up her dress to the small of her back. She still not looking at me—she just watching that show on incest. And I look at her fat thick thighs. And I slowly pull down her cotton Carters, they're all holey, pee-stained, elastic gone. She never spends money on herself—wouldn't buy herself a new pair of panties. No, that's my mama. I pull down her panties and I look at her fat rumpled ass like a piece of uncooked bacon. My hands soothe her dimpled flesh. I knead into her rear like I'm making bread. My mama! My mama, sweet, sweet mama.

Then I mount my own mama in the ass. That's right, I fuck my own mama in the ass, cause I'd never fuck my mama in her snatch! She's my mama.

I cum real quick. Cuz I'm a quick working man. Work real fast. After I cum, I cum outta my mama. I want my mama to want me but she don't ever want me. She still just watching that TV. Just suckin' that Pall Mall. So I know what I want to do. I want my sauce back. So I go down on my mama and suck my own cum outta my own mama's ass, outta her butthole. Gotta mouthful of her own coconut juice. Suck it out. Suck it. Pucker, pucker.

When I get a mouthful of that stuff, after I felch her good, I move my hands to my mama's face. I touch her red hair with its white streaks at the temples. Her potato face. I can see the raspberry lipstick leak into the wrinkles of her skin. That space between her lips and her nose. What's that space called? And I gently take the cigarette out of my mama's mouth cause if I got it wet she'd BEAT THE HELL OUTTA ME! SHE'D BEAT THE HELL OUTTA ME. I gently unseal my mama's lips and press my lips to my mama's. From the corner of her mouth I spit my cum back into her mouth. Like pearls from an oyster returning to the sea at last.

She just swallows the cum and says, "Boy, you got lazy ass cum. Just like your father. Your cum ain't salty. You can cum on my pancakes anytime."

REFRIGERATOR

AND THE FIRST—and the first—And the first memory, memory I have—I have of my father, the first memory I have of my father is him putting me into the refrigerator. He'd take off all of the clothes on my five-year-old body and I'd be naked, sitting on that silver rack in the icebox. My feet and fingers would get into the picalilli, they'd get into the mustard, the mayo—you wonder why I puke whenever I see any condiments—never enjoy my food. Gotta upchuck, gotta puke. And I got all my dollies around me. I'm holding on to all of my dollies. My arms hold on to my Barbie and Ken, my Aunt Jemima, my G.I. JOE, my Winnie-the-Pooh—all my dollies would protect me. All my prophets, princesses, and kings would stay with me.

Then my daddy is laughin'. Then my daddy is playin'. Then my daddy is gigglin' and smilin'. Don't you know I hate smiles and laughter. Don't you know I hate good times! 'Cause the only feelings I feel are NO NO NO feelings at all.

My daddy stands behind the icebox door. He's smiling wide, saying we're goin' play a secret game for just me and daddy. Then he say never tell anyone. It's just our game. IT'S JUST OUR GAME. IT'S JUST OUR LITTLE LITTLE GAME.

He slap slap. He slap slap. I don't know this game. I don't want to play this game. Then he smile wide. I hold on to my dollies more. Then he leans down to the vegetable bin, opens it and takes out the carrots, the celery, the zucchini, the cucumbers. Then he starts working on my little hole, my little little, hole. My little girl hole. Showing me what it's like to be a mama, he says. Showing me what it's like to be a woman. To be loved.

"That's a Daddy's job" he tells me. Working my little hole. Hee HEE HEHH-HEEE.

HEE HUHUHUHUH. Working my little hole hee hee hee. Working my little hole hee hee hee.

Next thing I know I'm in bed crying, bleeding. I got all my dollies and animals around me. And I've got Band-Aids between their legs. They couldn't

protect me so I'LL PROTECT THEM. If you can't be there for me—I'll always be there for you. I'll always, I'll always be there for you.

Then I hear my mama come home. And she starts yelling at me at the top of her lungs. "Whatever happened to the vegetables for the dinner, for tonight's dinner? Whatever happened to the dinner? You been playing with your food again, girl? I was going to make your father's favorite."

And I just want to scream out, but of course I can't, "Mama, open up your eyes! DON'T YOU KNOW THAT I'M DADDY'S FAVORITE!"

And I just cry to myself. Is this what it's like to be a mama? Oh, no. Is this what it's like to be a daddy? Oh, no. It's just being part of the whole human race. Shush, now. Shush. Shush, child, shush.

ACCORDING TO MY grandmother, Al Capone was present the night she went into labor with my father. My paternal grandfather was from a wealthy family that owned farms, dairies, orchards, department stores, gas stations. But he wasn't content just being a well-off Wisconsin gentleman.So, during

8

A SUGGESTION OF MADNESS

Prohibition, he started a prosperous bootlegging concern and began doing business with Capone.

My father's family was a family of adventurers. When my grandfather was a child, he and his parents and sister were the first family to cross the United States in an automobile. The story was captured in National Geographic. These were people who did big things, took risks. They lived on a grand scale. They owned lakes and islands in northern Wisconsin, and they lived a lot of their lives outdoors, roughing it. The Finleys said that they were related to both the Barrymores and the Joyces (as in James Joyce). Whether it was true or not doesn't matter as much as the fact that they believed it.

And then there was the madness, the despair, the mania, the headaches—the intense headaches genetically related to bipolar disorder, headaches so maddening that they caused my great-grandfather to shoot himself in the head. My great-grandmother's depression in the wake of her husband's death was so great that she gave all of her property away. This depression, passed down through generations, has been a major ingredient of my own self-expression.

Like the rest of his family, my father, George Finley, was an adventurer, a boundary-pusher. He was extremely gifted, witty, charming, moody. In the 1950s, he was a professional jazz percussionist. He experimented with homosexual sex, drugs, and every other new experience that crossed his path. He developed a heroin addiction that was serious enough to land him in Lexington, the rehab center, after he stole my grandmother's checks and forged her signature in order to feed his habit.

With the emergence of rock and roll, and his illness, he gave up jazz. In order to make a living, he became a salesman. When he married my mother he "settled down," but he was never what you would call a conventional man.

My father inherited his family's illness, though not its money. He suffered from manic depression, or bipolar disorder, which is a genetic disease. Manic depression was not diagnosed during my father's

lifetime. Those who suffered from it were often, disastrously, diagnosed as paranoid schizophrenic. That is the diagnosis my father received. He killed himself when he was forty-eight. I was twenty-one.

When I was fourteen, I had recurring dreams in which my father committed suicide. In the dream, my uncle came over with a Burger King dinner after my father killed himself, and I asked the police who was going to clean up the mess. This dream was upsetting both for its content and for the fact that it kept repeating itself—it recurred every night for a week. On the fourth night, I couldn't stand it anymore and I confronted my father about it. I still shudder when I recall telling him and him looking at me, emotionless and frozen, as if he was trying to hide something. He didn't deny the implication of the dream. Later, in real life, my uncle did come over with Burger King after the tragedy, and I did ask who was going to clean up the mess. In some ways this psychic premonition comforted me after the suicide. It seemed to indicate that there was some larger order to things, some explanation, and that thought gave me some relief.

Psychic phenomenon, predictions, omens, herbs, signs, tea leaves, auras, dreams, prophecies, and visions were all a part of my growing up. I was taught to read cards by my mother and her mother, who was Hungarian Gypsy. When my relatives visited, palms were read in a no-nonsense fashion. In 1978, when I went home for Christmas break, I read my father's palm. I looked for his lifeline and he said to me, "I don't have a lifeline, I have a deadline." He killed himself later that week.

He went into the garage, laid a piece of cardboard from a vacuum cleaner box on the floor, and put the gun to his temple. It was January, Friday the thirteenth. My ten-year-old brother, Brian, found my father dead in the garage. He had gone to get a shovel to clear a neighbor's walk. My forty-five-year-old mother was left with four sons and two daughters to bring up.

I went to our family seer, Harriet, the day my father died. He'd been acting angry and withdrawn, and none of the priests, doctors, and psychiatrists we'd gone to had been able to help. I didn't know what to do for him. When I entered Harriet's room and she looked up and saw me, she asked me to sit down and told everyone else in the room to leave. She poured me a brandy and told me that I couldn't help my father, that "everything" was "done." But she wouldn't tell me any more. I became agitated. She said that when I got home I would be greeted by a black man and a white woman. It was 3 P.M. She asked me to stay until 3:30.

When I got to my family's door, I was greeted by a black man and a white woman—the police. Seeing them standing there, just as Harriet had predicted, sent me into a state of shock. They told me that my father had committed suicide at 3:30.

My father's death gave me passion, an emotional indicator toward which to push the content of my work. It compelled me to take the unanswered grief, the terrible sadness that I lived with, and throw it at the world. It was the event that catapulted me into my heroic complex, my vision of myself as a kind of Joan of Arc. Because no one was

Performing A Suggestion of Madness *with Andy Soma*

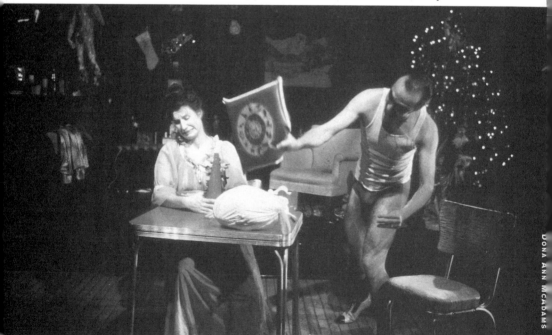

DONA ANN MCADAMS

A DIFFERENT KIND OF INTIMACY

able to protect me, I would protect others, be a do-gooder, lay the moral compass for others to live up to.

I CREATED A multimedia performance for the 10th anniversary of my father's suicide, in 1988. The piece, A *Suggestion of Madness*, consisted of a short play about a dysfunctional family and a short comic monologue. I had a nude dance troupe perform between acts. I ended the show by reading my father's suicide note.

I am interested in exposing devices and artifice, and, by reading this incredibly private document, I was trying to expose the absurdity of the idea that the theater can truly represent emotional pain, that it can cause the audience to experience emotions that are "real." It was my response to the concept of method acting.

DONA ANN McADAMS   *Jennifer Monson and The Dance Troupe.*

Act 1 Scene2 - description

Enter Louie: Slicked. He is the worstof the 50's and
60's and the 70's. It has recently been Christmas but not ~~too~~
too recent for most of the needles on the tree are off. ~~They~~
There is a purple curtain --almost like the purple shrouds
used to cover the statues at Lent in Catholic Churches.
Mary, Louie's wife sits making Christmas trees out of

macaroni. There is artificial snow everywhere. And thereis
only blue light. There is age middle age--
They are old enough to know the depressin, the 2nd
World War yet young enough to know Psychedelia.

Action

Louie: *forget, w/ audience ...* *on jul*
MARY, YOU LOOK MISERABLE MARY
I never knew you were so miserable, Mary.
(looks at her and changes voice)
But it is impossible to rescue you from from your misery
when it is misery you crave most of all.

Mary: Dear, I always smile when I think of thewife
as private property or the marriage laws written by man--   *sent*
or GOD in the image of man. You know why there are no   *of*
miracles in this world?cause God is you! Cause God is
in your image- the image of man-Noah- Abrahaham Moses -
Jesus - Mohammad - Santa Claus - Jimmy Swaggart - Cardinal
O'coonor. Yes, I think about history! As in Athens
the injured husband was personally allowed to kill his
unfaithful wife.

Louie: That's a long time ago Please, please don't
bring up the story of Karl Bodmer.

Mary: I will. You, have brought me to this point.   *I Follow*
There are paintings by Karl Bodmer, one of the earliest   *MARY*
painters of the West who travelled with Prince Maximillan
to the Upper missouri in 1833 and painted the Mandan
Indians. Four years later the entire tribe was wiped
out by smallpox.

Louie: Maybe they were IV users or practiced sodomy.
Hee, I shouldn't of said that. I'm sorry Mary. I   *TURN*
shouldn't of said that. I forgot about your sister.   *BACK*
(gets on knees) Please let me satisfy you. You never
let me satisfy you. You never let me give you joy

Mary: Look at you. Look at you. The Big Guy. Don't   *TURN*
you realize I sold my soul a long time ago to be your   *at AUD*
wife, the caretaker of your children. You see, I'm
immortal - So, dealing with you,the devil,is easy.
I have no identity, no property, no name of my own. I
have nothing to lose. Today, I woke up to the idea that

I'^dleave you in 1988. Today, I am bringing my sister who is
suffering from Modern Plague, living with Modern Plague
in this house. In this house for us to take care of her.

Louie: You wouldn't do that - The property values would drop.
Everyone at work ~~would~~ will shun me. I'll be scrutini-
nized - They'll burn our house down -I love your sister-
I even knocked her up once upon a time - Osterized ~~isn't going to be a word between whip and puree~~ —anymore— surely.
you can't do this to us. I've worked for 20 years breaking
my back in a job that only gives me stress and bad
ɑbreath -- I've never cried a single tear in my entire
manhood - I've hated everyone different than myself -
I can't take it! I just can't take it!

Mary: She's upstairs.

Louie: No! ~~This is middle America.~~ This white clean
pureMr,CleanGlenCovepo; luxeMicrowavereadytoseverreadyto
wearlife. Don't you destr y my indestructable, plastic
wrap, hefty trash bag lifestyle..I want to stay uninformed,
uninvolved, just follow the orders. You know why I like
Ollie North cause he's just like us. Follows the orders.
Never questions. Works for greed, lust, power, never
thinks about anyone elses lifestyle has any merit. I
know I live in a prison. But, don't bring your dying
siser in this house to make me feel. I don't want to feel.
I only want to feel the sensation of prick, the wad in
my wallet and to still believe that America will dominate th
the world.

Mary: Look at this as an opportunity to change. You'll
feel humility where you once felt pride. You'll feel compassion where you once felt prejudice. And you'll learn
to love in true meaning "love your neighbor as yourself".
Blessed are the sick for we shall learn how to comfort from them
and love from them.

Break in Energy

SUICIDE NOTE

by George Finley

I offer my hand my best one
That has not touched or cared for-
The dark hidden secrets of any soul

The hand sees The beating heart
like all hearts.
The mind sending up Thoughts
like all minds.
The blood flowing + bringing nourishment
like all blood.
This hand sees beyond temperment
+ torment, ideals language + culture,
But This hand has stopped feeling
the powerful search, The reaching within
This hand can hold + not be held
can be led but not lead
My light has darkened.
I stand naked as a day hawk
This is my destiny I must go.

A DIFFERENT KIND OF INTIMACY

To know I have hurt you is to
know that I would gladly bear
your pain.
To know that you have ever
been afraid of me is my
darkness of night.
No sun ever.
No infinity

WHEN MY MOTHER, Mary Steinert, was six months old, the steering wheel came off into her father's lap while the family was out for a drive. My mother's arm was nearly severed, and a piece of the windshield embedded itself in her

9

THE BLACK SHEEP

fontanelle. Her mother refused to let her arm be amputated. My mother was in a body cast for two years.

My maternal grandfather, Eddy, was a dashing gambler. He would take my mother with him on his gambling sprees to the Blackstone Hotel on Balboa Street, in Chicago. My grandfather's gambling addiction meant that it was not unusual for my mother to come home and find the furniture or other household items gone, sold, or repossessed. She lived with the awareness that everything might be gone at any time.

My father had red hair and freckled white skin, but my mother was olive-complexioned. Dark. My brothers believed that she was black when they were young. I remember going to Wisconsin to visit my father's family, and the people at restaurants asking the squaw with the long black braid to enter in the back. Sometimes, my mother was mistaken for a domestic, the nanny of her own children. She was constantly asked about her skin, about where she came from. How did she keep a tan all year?

On her father's side, my mother was Eastern-European, of Jewish descent (though her ancestors had converted to Catholicism). On her mother's side, in addition to being Hungarian Gypsy, my mother was American Indian. My mother did not appear to be white. Because of that, she made sure that we lived in an integrated neighborhood. My mother felt more comfortable around people of color. And she blended in more in integrated neighborhoods than she did in WASPy ones. She wasn't stigmatized outright, because in society's eyes she occupied some fuzzy zone between "colored" and "white," but she lived with a shame of her skin, her darkness, and of being eroticized because of her "exotic" looks. The last thing she said to me, just before she died, was that the first thing she was going to talk to God about was "skin color."

Mental illness was present in my mother's family as well as my father's. My maternal grandmother suffered from depression and schizophrenia. On one visit to my grandmother's when I was very small, she insisted we all wear bathing caps to protect us from the rays of the aliens next door. Eventually my mother had to have her committed.

My mother's father died suddenly, of pneumonia, one weekend when she was ten. Her mother was five months pregnant. Mary soon went to work washing floors and working in a bakery. Her life was one of poverty and of too much responsibility for her age. It is her pain I have cried out in my art—the pain of the child who is not taken care of and so becomes the caretaker.

With great suffering comes either a bitterness or knowledge, a heightened sensitivity, a greater goodness. My mother had that sensitivity and goodness. If someone in our home kicked a door, she would say, "Don't kick the door. It is a tree."

She was an activist. On hot, windy nights, when trucks sprayed DDT on trees, my mother would stand outside measuring the winds, to gauge the amount of pesticide dispersed. She was insistent on the issue of civil rights, and if anyone ever made a racist remark, even in jest, they were immediately thrown out of our house.

I asked her once how she coped with missing my father, her husband, after his death. How she coped with being left alone.

"I would sit in restaurants and see families together. I would see families with fathers, in cars, on vacations, celebrating, and I would ask God why my family wasn't intact, why I couldn't be in one of those families. But finally I encountered my pain, my pride—the sin of pride. The sin of envy. And now when I see families—mothers and fathers—together, I am happy that that feeling of family exists, that it is out there. It isn't something I have to have, own. But it exists. And when I see people happy, I am not envious of their happiness. I feel happy for them and with them."

That became my motivation—the remarkable way in which my mother was able to transform her pain into compassion. That was what I wanted to do with my art.

The idea of turning pain into compassion was something that applied in a very direct way to my public sculpture, *The Black Sheep*.

I wrote "The Black Sheep," the poem that concludes The Theory of Total Blame, as a prayer for the disenfranchised in society, for the Other. It is my version of "The Lord Is My Shepherd . . ."

At the opening of "The Black Sheep," on a corner at First and Houston Streets in lower Manhattan, a man came up to me and told me how much he liked the sculpture. "You know it is sitting right on top of my house? I wake up to it every day." I realized that this man lived in the subway. And I was overwhelmed by the realization that my art couldn't really do anything to fix his life—that life is more important than art, but life is meaningless without art.

1st Ave at ___

St Marks

Black Sheep of Society

DONA ANN MCADAMS

THE BLACK SHEEP

After a funeral someone said to me
You know I only see you at funerals
it's been 3 since June—
been five since June for me.
He said I've made a vow—
I only go to death parties if I knew someone
before they were sick.
Why?
cause—cause—cause I feel I feel so
sad cause I never knew their lives
and now I only know their deaths
And because we are members of the
Black Sheep family.

We are sheep with no shepherd
We are sheep with no straight and narrow
We are sheep with no meadow
We are sheep who take the dangerous pathway through
the mountain range
to get to the other side of our soul.
We are the black sheep of the family
called Black Sheep folk.
We always speak our mind.
     appreciate differences in culture
     believe in sexual preferences
     believe in no racism
     no sexism
     no religionism
and we'll fight for what we believe

but usually we're pagans.

There's always one in every family.

Even when we're surrounded by bodies

we're always alone.

You're born alone

and you die alone—

written by a black sheep.

You can't take it with you—

written by a former black sheep.

Black Sheep folk look different from their families—

The way we look at the world.

We're a quirk of nature—

We're a quirk of fate.

Usually our family, our city,

our country doesn't understand us—

We knew this from when we were very young

that we weren't meant to be understood.

That's right. That's our job.

Usually we're not appreciated until the next generation.

That's our life. That's our story.

Usually we're outcasts, outsiders in our own family.

Don't worry—get used to it.

My sister says—I don't understand you!

But I have many sisters with me tonight.

My brother says—I don't want you!

But I have many brothers with me here tonight!

My mother says—I don't know how to love

someone like you!

You're so different from the rest!

But I have many mamas with me here tonight!

My father says—I don't know how to hold you!

But I have many daddies with me here tonight!

We're related to people we love who can't say

      I love you Black Sheep daughter

      I love you Black Sheep son

      I love you outcast, I love you outsider.

But tonight we love each other

That's why we're here—

to be around others like ourselves—

So it doesn't hurt quite so much.

In our world, our temple of difference

I am at my loneliest when I have something to celebrate

and try to share it with those I love

who don't love me back.

There's always silence at the end

of the phone.

There's always silence at the end

of the phone.

Sister—congratulate me!

NO I CAN'T YOU'RE TOO LOUD—

Grandma—love me!

NO I DON'T KNOW HOW TO LOVE

SOMEONE LIKE YOU

Sometimes the Black Sheep is a soothsayer,

a psychic, a magician of sorts.

Black Sheep see the invisible—

We know each other's thoughts—

We feel fear and hatred.

Sometimes some sheep are chosen to be sick

      to finally have average, flat, boring people say

      I love you.

Sometimes Black Sheep are chosen to be sick

      so families can finally come together and say

I love you.

Sometimes some Black Sheep are chosen to die

so loved ones and families can finally say

Your life was worth living

Your life meant something to me!

Black Sheeps' destinies are not necessarily in having families,

having prescribed existences—

like the American Dream.

Black Sheep's Destinies are to give meaning in life

to be angels

to be conscience

to be nightmares

to be actors in dreams.

Black Sheep can be family to strangers

We can love each other like MOTHER

FATHER SISTER BROTHER CHILD

We understand universal love

We understand unconditional love.

We feel a unique responsibility

a human responsibility, for feelings for others.

We can be all things to all people

We are three at 3:30 AM when you call

We are here tonight cause I just can't go to sleep.

I have nowhere else to go.

I'm a creature of the night—

I travel in your dreams—

I feel your nightmares—

We are your holding hand

We are your pillow, your receiver,

your cuddly toy.

I feel your pain.

I wish I could relieve you of your suffering.

I wish I could relieve you of your pain.

I wish I could relieve you of your death.

But it's always

Silence at the end of the phone.

Silence at the end of the phone.

Silence at the end of the phone.

WHEN I WAS in high school, I started reading *Artforum* and the *Village Voice* for art reviews. I learned about Chris Burden, who was doing his famous early performances where he shot himself, locked himself in a locker for days. I thought he was brilliant. Vito Acconci was my other favorite. He did a

10

PUBLIC SUPPORT

piece called *Semen Bed* in the basement of the infamous Leo Castelli Gallery, where he sat on a bed, masturbating. There were women involved with this new kind of art, too. There was Yoko Ono, who had the audience at her performances snip pieces of her dress; and Charlotte Mormon, who played the cello nude.

These were the people I looked toward as mentors and masters. When I was growing up, in the sixties and seventies, their work was sanctioned by the academy, and, in a sense, protected by it. However one might label it—as performance, action, conceptual art—their art was part of a tradition, the tradition of art history. I wanted to be a part of that tradition, too.

THE NATIONAL ENDOWMENT for the Arts was founded in 1965, for the purpose of "creating and sustaining not only a climate encouraging freedom of thought, imagination and inquiry but also the material conditions facilitating the release of . . . creative talent." The NEA quickly became the single largest source of arts funding in the country. Moreover, private funders began to follow the NEA's lead in deciding what artists and programs to support. By 1990, through direct support, matching grants, and its leadership position, the NEA's decisions had the effect of directing approximately $1 billion a year.

The NEA gave disenfranchised American artists the power of "public support" for the first time. The National Endowment for the Arts was funding work by those who were once rendered invisible by economic, ethnic, or gender differences. What previously had been a private, almost sequestered world, existing only within academia or in galleries, became public. People who had never had the same access that white, middle- or upper-class men have traditionally had, were suddenly given the means to create.

Those who had once been disembodied voices became visible and claimed a place on the public stage. In the 1980s, David Wojnarowicz could write frankly about what it was like to be a gay man, instead of closeting his work as Tennessee Williams and

Truman Capote had done. He could shuck off the stereotypes that gay artists had once been forced to hide behind, for fear of threatening their heterosexual patrons. Once, modernists like Picasso and Braque co-opted African art traditions, while the work of the African artists themselves was placed in the Museum of Natural History. But now, artists like Adrian Piper and David Hammons could demand to be seen in the same context as the modernists. They could challenge western ideas of beauty, or make confrontational work about racism. Women could go beyond the mothers-and-children subject matter of artists like Mary Cassatt, or they could attack that subject in a new and discomfiting way, as Sally Mann did.

These changes were obviously due to cultural shifts that happened over the course of decades, but they were also due, in no small part, to the contributions of the NEA. Because of the funding that the NEA provided through institutions and programs, artists were able to critique culture from the inside. But then there was a backlash.

Art as transgression, or any transgressive act, becomes a Rorschach test for the culture it comes out of. In one sense, transgressive art is a kind of psychic problem-solving, at the cultural level. It looks head-on at unresolved hostilities, humiliations, traumas. It offers catharsis—and you could say that it's only in the aftermath of catharsis that healing is possible. But if the culture is not ready to face those hostilities, humiliations, traumas, then it responds with tremendous anxiety—anxiety which is expressed as hostility toward the artist.

What was happening in the eighties and nineties with the cultural response to "transgressive" art was the acting out of a tremendous reservoir of fear.

NINETEEN-EIGHTY-NINE was when the right wing's attacks on artistic freedom and freedom of expression began in earnest. Two NEA-funded artists, Robert Mapplethorpe and Andres Serrano, came to the attention of conservatives in Congress. Mapplethorpe's exhibit "The Perfect Moment," at the Institute of Contemporary Art in

Philadelphia, had been funded with money that the Institute had received from the NEA. The exhibit contained photographs that were considered homoerotic and pornographic—words that were interchangeable in the minds of the Republicans in Congress. Serrano, who had been awarded $15,000 by an organization that received NEA support, had produced the famous Piss Christ—a photograph of a crucifix immersed in urine.

This was the kind of issue that Senator Jesse Helms, Republican of North Carolina—formerly a staunch opponent of the Civil Rights Movement, and a supporter of the idea that HIV-positive people should be put in internment camps—could really sink his teeth into. Helms became the ringleader of a group of conservatives in Congress who began agitating, in the press and on the floor of the House, for an amendment to the NEA's grant-evaluation procedure.

The proposed amendment would prohibit the NEA from funding work that was obscene or offensive to taxpayers. (The anti-NEA team referred to these "taxpayers" again and again over the course of the controversy that was to follow. It was as if they thought that the only people who paid taxes were the people who voted for them.)

The original criteria by which NEA grant applications were to be evaluated had been established in 1965. Those criteria were extremely broad: "professional excellence," etc. But when the time came to consider the NEA's appropriations for fiscal year 1990, Congress enacted an amendment that revised the criteria by which grants were to be awarded. The amendment said that the NEA could only fund work which did not "promote, disseminate, or produce materials which in the judgement of the NEA may be considered obscene, including but not limited to depictions of sadomasochism, homoeroticism, the sexual exploitation of children . . . " The NEA implemented this amendment by requiring all artists who received grants to sign a clause stating that they would abide by Congress's criteria. (This amendment remained in place until 1991, when it was struck down in federal court.)

But this clause was not enough for Congressional conservatives, many of whom began calling for the complete abolishment of the NEA. They created an "Independent Commission" of constitutional scholars to assess their options for quote-unquote "revising the grant-making procedures." In my opinion, they were hoping to get a constitutional green light to revise the NEA right out of existence.

The controversy snowballed. The director of Cincinnati's Contemporary Art Center was indicted for mounting a show of Robert Mapplethorpe's photographs. Members of Donald Wildman's group, the American Family Association, went to Franklin Furnace posing as art historians in order to gain access to David Wojnarowicz's files. The imposters photocopied Wojnarowicz's work. They then reassembled the most "obscene" parts into a collage in which the images were literally taken completely out of context. Wildman used this bizarre visual aid to raise money for his cause. I find it surreal that a man like this could stand up and accuse other people of immorality. Wojnarowicz sued Wildman and eventually won the case. He was awarded one dollar.

There was fear in the art community. Artists would hold meetings to talk about what was happening and to discuss strategies for dealing with it. One of the first things I remember being told was, "Make sure you pay your taxes and keep all of your financial files in order." People remembered how anti-war organizations in the 1960s were constantly audited by the IRS. It was one of the tactics the government used to drain the vitality of those who opposed it. And sure enough, very soon, many of the most important alternative art spaces in the country were being audited.

I N 1987, A sixteen-year-old African-American female was found, dazed and semi-conscious, in a trash bag in an apartment complex in upstate New York. When she was found, she was covered in human excrement. The young woman's name was Tawana Brawley, and she said she had been raped by a group of white police officers.

11

WE KEEP OUR VICTIMS READY

The case quickly became national news, with a highly publicized investigation and trial. Through it all, accusations were made toward the young woman herself. Brawley was accused of faking the whole thing.

To this day there are many things about the story that aren't clear, but what was clear to me from the beginning was that Tawana Brawley was being exploited and abused. This young woman was not an adult; she was a juvenile, and the authorities should automatically have been protective of her. She had been missing from her home for days before she was found. Even if she did smear the feces on herself, the important thing to ask one's self was, who or what could make a young woman do something like that?

I couldn't get the image of the young woman smeared with feces out of my mind. To me, what had happened to Tawana Brawley seemed like some kind of biblical tale, but one where all the symbols and the meanings had been scrambled and confused. I decided to try to create a performance out of the chaos.

I knew that I could never go emotionally where Brawley had been, and I could not actually put real feces on myself. Even if I could bring myself to do it, it would disgust the audience so much that they wouldn't be able to focus on anything else. So I decided to use chocolate. It looked like shit. And I liked the idea of chocolate's history, its association with love.

In the piece that grew out of this, I smeared my body with chocolate, because, I said in the piece, I'm a woman, and women are usually treated like shit. Then I covered myself with red candy hearts—because, "after a woman is treated like shit, she becomes more lovable." After the hearts, I covered myself with bean sprouts, which smelled like semen and looked like semen—because, after a woman is treated like shit, and loved for it, she is jacked off on. Then I spread tinsel all over my body, like a Cher dress—because, no matter how badly a woman has been treated, she'll still get it together to dress for dinner.

Why can't this veal calf walk?

YOU SOLD MY SOUL BEFORE I COULD SPEAK
RAPED BY AN UNCLE AT 8
KNOWN ADDICTION all my lives
let me dance for you
my daddy was a preacher
preach the bible
       beat my mama —
then kiss' me
I sell my babies
I sell my bodies.

To keep 'em from stealing
the women had to strip and
had to work naked.
it looks bad
but to me it looks normal.

Why can't this veal calf walk?
cause she's kept in a wooden box.
That she can't turn around in.
She's fed some anti biotic laced
formula — and she sleeps in
her own diarreah — chained in
a darkened building — immobilized
& sick — and then we kill her
and eat her.

WE KEEP OUR
VICTIMS READY

ST. VALENTINE'S MASSACRE

I was afraid of being loved—
    so I loved being hated
I was afraid of being wanted—
    so I wanted to be abused
I was afraid of being alone—
    so I alone became afraid
I was afraid of being successful—
    so I successfully became nothing
I was afraid of not being in control—
    so I lost control of my own life
I was afraid that I was worth nothing—
    so I wasted my body to nothing
I was afraid of eating—
    so I eat to my heart's content
    so I drink to my heart's content
        I party to my heart's content
        I fuck to my heart's content
        I spend to my heart's content
        I eat to my heart's content
        and then I puke it all up
            I take laxatives
            and shit and shit and shit and shit
        I'm afraid I shit a long time
        for I'm nothing but shit
        My life is worth nothing but shit.

I've had my share of love letters.

I'm writing to tell you that I love you but I don't ever

want to see you again.

I never want to talk to you again, hear your voice, smell you, touch you, hold
you.

I want you out of my life, I love you but I want you out of my life! But remember,
I will never love anyone as much as I love you!

I'm beating you with this belt, this whip, this stick

because I love you.

You talked back to me and your mother. Your bloody back, your scars, are

evidence of my love.

I beat you as a child because I loved you.

The only emotion I ever saw from my parents was anger.

I'm sleeping with your best friend because

I want to make you jealous

and make you realize that you love me.

I make you jealous because I love you.

I sleep with your best friend because I love you.

I am hurting you because I love you.

I ignore you because I don't want you to know that I

love you till you show me that you love me. I ignore you

because I love you.

I tied your hands together as a child because you were

touching your penis too much. I tied up your penis

because I love you.

I put you down as a child because I didn't want you to

expect too much out of life. I ridiculed you, I belittled you because I loved you.

I abused my children sexually because I didn't want
someone else who didn't love them to do it. I don't hate
them, I love them. I show them love.

I shot myself because I love you.
If I loved myself I'd be shooting you.

I drink myself to death because I never loved myself.
I love you. But I love my liquor more.

Yes, I know love. That is the reason I hate the people
I love.
My whole life is untangling what was hate and what was love.
My whole life is falling in love with those who hate me while loving me.
I always fall in love with the cruel, the sadistic
For it's better to feel abuse than to feel nothing at all.
It's better to feel abuse than to feel nothing at all.

WHY CAN'T THIS VEAL CALF WALK?
You sold my soul before I could speak.

Raped by an uncle at eight
Known addiction all my life
Let me dance for you
My daddy was a preacher
Preached the bible
Beat my mama
I sell my babies
I sell my bodies.

To keep 'em from stealing the women had to strip and had to work naked. It
looks bad, but to me it looks normal.

Why can't this veal calf walk?

'Cause she's kept in a wooden box which she can't turn around in. She's fed

some antibiotic-laced formula,

and she sleeps in her own diarrhea,

chained in a darkened building, immobilized and sick

and then we kill her and eat her.

After I was raped by my doctor

I didn't want to be close to anyone.

I cut off my hair

I cut off my breasts

I cut off my hips

I cut off my buttocks

     nothing revealing, nothing tight

     neutered.

You say I got what I deserved

I let the doctor examine my crotch

My legs were in the stirrups pinned down

And you gave me a shot

I couldn't see you but I could feel you. I couldn't do nothing.

Everyone always told me I couldn't do nothing my whole life

Just seeing the veal calf now.

Everyone says I deserved it—

I'm a hussy, I'm a tramp

I'm a whore

'Cause I wear lipstick?

work at night?

and drink bourbon straight?

I'm a preacher girl

Daddy, teach me right.

When I said NO

you didn't listen to me.

When I said NO

You fucked me anyway

When I said NO

I meant no

When I said NO

I wasn't playing hard to get

And I never meant yes

You raped me

I took a shower, a hot one

but I couldn't get clean

    his sweat his semen

    his skin smells near

Another bath another shower

my whole body was covered with hickeys

I just cried, I just cried.

When I reported it

Policeman said, "Hey, slut, you led him on."

The doctor cleaned me up, stuffed me with gauze

I bled three days with the morning-after pill.

And when they returned my empty wallet

Mr. Policeman said, "If you don't suck me I'll blow your brains out."

GET ME USED TO IT! GET ME USED TO IT!

But I can't. I want something better for my sisters my

daughters. And every day I hear them laughing at me

from street corners. Sizing me up. They don't say it,

though, when I walk down the street with a man 'cause then I'm his property.

And the menfolk say as I pass—

    I prefer small women

    I like to dominate women

    I enjoy the conquest of sex

Some women are asking for it
I get excited when a woman struggles
I'd like to make it with her
I hope I score tonight.

And when the last man said his violence
I knew I couldn't do anything to them
so I'd do something to me.
I went and took a knife and I cut out my hole
but it just became a bigger hole
and all the men just laughed and said
She's too big to fuck now
And I felt relief, but then they said,
We can all fuck her at the same time.
But I was bleeding so they left me alone
Men don't touch women when they bleed
It's unclean, unless they cause the bleeding.

And then I hoped I would die but of course I didn't
I heard a sound, a whimper
and I realized I was in the same room as the veal calf
And veal calf walked over to me
Veal calf limps. Veal calf stinks.
And I look into veal calf's eyes
And I know veal calf's story
And I said I was sorry for her
And she said I got to keep trying
And she asked why I was there, too
And I spoke my story:

When the big man like a big daddy like a big uncle, big uncle whom I loved,
when the cop, the teacher, the country doctor, the neighbor, the authority man
whom I trusted and respected visited me in my own bed, broke into my own

house, lived with me, on my own street in my own car, looked at me, grabbed me, mangled and hurt me, slapped me and pushed me, touched my privacy, destroyed my feminine instinct, entered and took and hurt and screams and bruises, new colors on my skin . . .
Whenever I see a rainbow in the sky I only see an angel being raped.

When I said NO I meant No
But you did it anyway
When you were gone your body, your stink remained
Tried to wash you wash you off me, my body, my skin in me in me in me
Wash it off me, still not gone, scrub it off, burn you off me
Try to kill me, I don't like me, 'cause I smell like you.

I'm hurt, abused. I slice me.
I burn me. I hit me. I want this body to die. I want to be
old and undesired.
I want my body back—
        society, culture and history
        media, entertainment and art
I'm more than a hole
But you hate us because we can have babies and you
can't.
I'm more than a hole
But you envy us because we have children who
love us unconditionally.
I'm more than a set of tits
But if I don't have the right size for you
I'm never enough for you
So, we make implants and surgery just for you.
We create a woman that never existed.
It's survival of the female species.
And I'm more than a pair of legs
But if they don't do more than walk

I'm a dog.

If I nurse my babies and my tits sag

And I'm told you won't desire me

You can't be a mother and a whore

No one loves a smart woman

I'm more than a piece of ass, a good fuck and lay

For the woman—our society only relates and values

you for your desirability.

The Woman is Private Property.

DONA ANN McADAMS

A DIFFERENT KIND OF INTIMACY

DONA ANN McADAMS

THE TELEVISION WAS black-and-white, but we knew the blood flowing out of the young man's head was scarlet. The policeman kept pounding the skull with skill and determination. The camera panned in for a close-up and my stomach shuddered in revulsion.

It was August, 1968. I was having a slumber party. At first my friends and I thought

POLITICS

12

we were seeing a movie. But soon, we learned that it was the Chicago Democratic Convention. We stood mesmerized, forgetting Amy's bra in the freezer. Nineteen-sixty-eight was the year of assassinations, the Civil Rights movement, and the Vietnam War. We had already become used to society's rage. But this was worse somehow, maybe because it was so close to home.

Seeing the demonstrators beaten was my entrance into the counterculture's rage and the unrest of the entire nation. My personal anger, hostility, and anxiety had found a context in which it felt at home.

The Chicago Democratic Convention produced the Chicago 7. I went to Evanston City Hall when I was still in junior high, to see the defendants and their attorney, William Kunstler, speak. Kunstler later formed the Center for Constitutional Rights, which would handle the NEA 4 trial, in which I was a plaintiff. The lead attorney for the NEA case was David Cole, Kunstler's protégé. David Cole was from Evanston. When I found this out, it seemed like an odd coincidence.

I APPLIED FOR a solo artist's grant from the National Endownment for the Arts for 1990. While the application was pending, I performed "We Keep Our Victims Ready" at the Walker Art Center in Minneapolis. I received a positive evaluation from the NEA panel-member who came to see my show.

The process for recieving an NEA grant is a lengthy one. You submit a curriculum vitae, an artist's statement, and examples of work. If you have applied for a theater grant (as I had), a local theater professional comes to see you perform. You then meet with a local peer panel for an interview. The peer panel sends a recommendation, either for approval or denial of the grant, to the 26-member National Council on the Arts in Washington, DC.

The Council convenes to review the applications recommended for approval by the national peer panels. Then the Council's recommendations are sent to the NEA's chairman for approval. These last two steps are really a formality. In the history of the NEA, peer panel recommendations have rarely been overturned.

My peer panel review went well that year. I was recommended for approval.

But sometime in early May, 1990, someone went into my application files and leaked information about "We Keep Our Victims Ready" to the widely syndicated conservative columnists Rowland Evans and Robert Novak. I was about to become the latest casualty of the so-called culture wars.

That year, the National Council was to convene to review peer panel recommendations on the weekend of May 12–13. On May 11, Rowland and Evans's column, entitled "New 'Art' Storm Brewing," appeared in the *Washington Post*, the *New York Post*, and other major dailies across America.

In the column, Evans and Novak wrote that the chairman of the NEA, John Frohnmeyer, had been advised by unnamed "friends" to veto a number of solo-artist grant applications up for review. Among the applications was that of a "chocolate smeared young woman" — me. A Frohnmeyer veto would "ease President Bush's deepening troubles with conservatives on his suspect cultural agenda," wrote Evans and Novak. Approval of the grants, on the other hand, would make it difficult for Bush to "defuse the hottest cultural-and-taxpayer issue out in the land beyond the Beltway."

This thinly veiled threat did the trick. The Council neither rejected nor approved the eighteen contested theater applications that weekend. It decided to postpone its decision until after "more information" about the artists and their work could be obtained.

I was outraged by the Evans and Novak piece, and I wrote a response, which was published on May 19 in the *Washington Post*. I pointed out that Evans and Novak's portrayal of me as the "chocolate smeared young woman" was grossly reductive, and created the erroneous impression that my work was sexual in nature. I tried to present a more balanced picture of my career, and I said that I felt Evans and

Novak's attack was "part of a larger trend of supressing artists — especially those whose work deals with difficult social issues — by playing on society's fears, prejudices, and problems."

On June 20, 1990, the "additional information" on the eighteen contested grants was sent to the members of the Council. A week later, at a meeting of an artists' organization in Seattle, John Frohnmeyer said that "political realities" would probably mean that some grants would be vetoed.

One of the "political realities" Frohnmeyer was referring to may have been a short letter addressed to him, from George Bush, dated June 19. "I do not want to see censorship," Bush wrote, "yet I don't believe a dime of taxpayer's [sic] money should go into art that is clearly and visibly filth . . . . The taxpayer will not subsidize filth and patently blasphemous material. You are doing a good job and I support you. Keep it up!"

Frohnmeyer — a mild-mannered, environmentally conscious, L.L. Bean–wearing Republican from Oregon — didn't have the stomach for this kind of thing. He conducted a cursory telephone poll of the Council members, and, on June 29, he announced that four of the eighteen grants had been vetoed. Mine was one of them. The others belonged to performance artists Holly Hughes, John Fleck, and Tim Miller. Needless to say, we were all devastated when we heard the news.

A coalition of artists, advocates, and attorneys decided that we four artists should band together and sue for reinstatement of the grants. Attorney Mary Dorman and arts advocate Joy Silverman, of the National Campaign for Freedom of Expression, and David Cole from the Center For Constitutional Rights (William Kunstler's organization), came on board to represent us. Mealne Verveer of People for the American Way steered the direction of the lawsuit. And of course, the ACLU joined in.

Meanwhile, the media was having a field day and the art community was in a frenzy. There were speeches, demonstrations, editorials, political meetings, debriefings, television shows, memos, inquiries. Jesse Helms brought my work up on the Senate floor as an example of why the NEA shouldn't be funded.

While all this was going on, I secluded myself in Nyack, New York, where Michael and I (married by this time) lived above a jewelry store. I was thankful for the smallness of the quaint town. Michael stood by me, being more than supportive. But there was only so much he could do. I was bitter at the thought that I had become the victim after all—from portraying one in my work to really becoming one. And I was afraid of the impact the NEA case would have on my career. I wanted to be known for my art, not as the anti-censorship queen.

TIMOTHY GREENFIELD-SANDERS

The chocolate-smeared woman poses for TIME

But I never considered not going ahead with the lawsuit. I felt a responsibility towards the importance of the case and seeing it through. I was aware that many people didn't think that withholding subsidies for artists was really censorship, and that they thought that I and my fellow artists were coddled, spoiled. I felt I had to demonstrate how wrong that was.

So, when the team of attorneys filed suit in the 9th Circuit in Los Angeles, I was one of the plaintiffs. The NEA 4 had been officially born. (The case became known as Finley et. al. vs. the NEA because my name happened to be the first, alphabetically, of the four.)

By now, the artists whose grants had been approved were receiving their official notifications of acceptance, along with the forms that required them to sign "the Helms clause"—the clause that stipulated that the artist could not create work with "homoerotic, sado-masochistic," or other "obscene" content. Most artists signed the clause. Some artists pointed out that the Helms Clause was eerily reminiscent of Nazi rhetoric and refused to sign.

Meanwhile, the Independent Commission had reported back to Congress. Acting on the commission's recommendations, Congress adopted the Williams/Coleman Amendment (better known as the "decency clause"), which directs the Chairperson of the NEA to "take into consideration general standards of decency and respect for the diverse beliefs and values of the American public." At that point, the NEA 4 were joined by a new plaintiff, the National Association of Artists' Organizations (NAAO). Our lawyers amended our complaint so that, in addition to suing for reinstatement of our grants, we were now challenging the constitutionality of the decency clause.

I was the only straight artist in the NEA 4 and I was portrayed in the press as the nice married girl who lives in a small town and does art. It was as if they felt it was necessary to use my nonthreatening personal life to say, "See? *Some* artists are decent." People from arts lobbying groups used to ask me if I would like to meet Jesse Helms for tea, to show him what a nice wholesome young woman I was. I said no. I didn't think my personality or sexual preference should have anything to do with whether or not I was protected by the First Amendment.

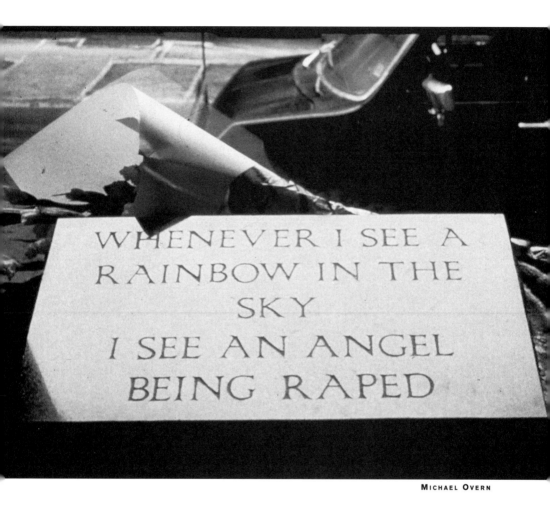

WHENEVER I SEE A
RAINBOW IN THE
SKY
I SEE AN ANGEL
BEING RAPED

MICHAEL OVERN

THE SPRING OF 1990 was busy—I had *We Keep Our Victims Ready*, I was working on *The Black Sheep*, the NEA conflict was brewing, and I had a one-woman show at Franklin Furnace. They were going to be hosting my first installation, which made me happy, because they had hosted my first performance in New York City almost ten years before.

13

A WOMAN'S LIFE ISN'T WORTH MUCH

Franklin Furnace, located in TriBeCa, was one of the most prestigious venues for performance and installation in America. The director, Martha Wilson, also curated one of the best collections of artist's books in any private institution. (The collection is now available in the library of the Museum of Modern Art.) Jenny Holzer and many other prominent artists got their starts there. It was a vibrant and exciting place.

For the installation, I painted the walls from floor to ceiling with texts in my own handwriting. The theme was abortion and women's isues. At this time abortion rights were being constantly threatened in Congress (as they are today), and the restrictions were tightening. I displayed books that I had redone in the style of Joe Orton. I had a two-story wall mural depicting the Virgin Mary, with the text "The Virgin Mary is Pro-Choice."

MICHAEL OVERN

The Virgin Mary is PRO-CHOICE

MICHAEL OVERN

Franklin Furnace had offices on the top floor, installations and artists' books on the ground floor, and a performance space in the basement. The night of my opening, another artist, Diane Torr, was performing in the basement. The next day, the fire department announced that the performance had occurred in violation of fire laws, and Franklin Furnace was closed. Performances had been going on in the basement for ten years and it was the first time they had had a problem. The top floor, with my installation, was re-opened, but the performance space never re-opened.

Tactics like fire-law closures and IRS audits had become routine, just as people had predicted they might. It was the right wing's method of putting pressure on small non-profit institutions whose budgets were already pushed to their limits. Franklin Furnace, the Kitchen, and other institutions that had shown or supported "degenerate" art were audited by the IRS. The pressure put on the boards and staff of such institutions was tremendous. This witch hunt caused many arts organizations to close their doors forever. And there was nothing to take their place.

And all the time, Helms and his henchmen were propagating the myth that artists, like the proverbial "welfare queens" of the inner cities, were living high on the hog at the government's expense, and that employees of these arts institutions were making big salaries. It was laughable. At that time, I had no health insurance and basically lived from hand to mouth. All I received for the Franklin Furnace installation, for instance, was a few hundred dollars and a set of keys to the building.

Many industries in this country receive government subsidies: agriculture, education, pharmacology, the space industry, and so on. Why shouldn't the art industry be subsidized? In most of the rest of the world, culture is looked at as food for the soul, and governments recognize that funding the arts is good for the economy, because it benefits the tourism, restaurant, and entertainment industries.

It takes a tremendous amount of energy and initiative to start and sustain a non-profit arts organization. When one of these organizations is forced to close its doors, all of that energy and initiative is lost. And it's not just "highbrow" organizations like Franklin Furnace that were shut down in the culture wars. Community arts organizations all around America were shuttered too. Young people in those communities will not have the opportunity to learn about the arts or their own creative capacities. This is a significant step back for American culture.

IN THE SUMMER of 1990, a demonstration was held at the Federal Building in Washington DC in connection with the NEA lawsuit. I gave a speech. While I was speaking, a man in the audience threw a glass of urine at me, probably in reaction to Piss Christ. The jar smashed and shards of glass went everywhere. I was covered in urine and I could have been seriously injured. Michael started to go after my attacker but Norman Siegel, head of New York ACLU, held him back. I felt like my entire life was being consumed with this political melodrama.

It was hard to remember sometimes that I was supposed to be an artist, not an activist—the distinction between the two was becoming blurrier and blurrier. Around this time, I was asked to host Dance Theater Workshop's annual Bessie Awards with the comedian Danitra Vance. I said yes, but then I discovered that the event was to be sponsored by Phillip Morris. Phillip Morris was also a major supporter of Jesse Helms. In good conscience, I felt I could not participate in the awards. I felt it was wrong for a corporation to try to play it both ways—courting liberal opinion in New York City and financing Jesse Helms's campaign in North Carolina.

The dance community was very against my pulling out, because Phillip Morris is such a big supporter of dance. A dance critic from the New York Times called me personally to tell me her feelings. This is a good example of what I call liberal convenient denial. The art community was letting itself be used by Philip Morris, which obviously is a fundamentally conservative organization no matter how much it supports avant-garde dance at the advice of its image consultants.

Danitra Vance pulled out as well. She had her own issues with Phillip Morris. She died of cancer the following year.

I CONCENTRATED ON MAKING work that focused attention on gay rights and gay issues. At the Painted Bride in Philadelphia I did an installation that included wedding cakes with figurines of same-sex couples, along with funereal wreaths for AIDS victims.

It was the height of the AIDS epidemic. Because of homophobia and ignorance,

14

A CERTAIN LEVEL OF DENIAL

many victims of the disease did not even receive proper funerals. Undertakers were afraid to handle the bodies, families were ashamed of the cause of death. There was no service, no wake, and the deceased person's friends had no way to express their grief. In response to this, the memorial service became commonplace. Friends and loved ones would come together to remember the deceased with speeches, slides, and so on. There were so many deaths that one service seemed to blend into the next. In my community there was the feeling of a constant funeral—a constant grieving. I lost many, many friends.

My friend the performer Ethyl Eichelberger took his life rather than let the disease run its course. Ethyl was a six-foot-tall drag queen, a brilliant actor and artist who had performed for Charles Ludlam. He created work where he combined classical dramatic texts with original material, and he had a wonderfully trained voice that he would use to switch in and out of different personae. We had performed together in the '80s at 8 B.C. He took a liking to me and encouraged me as a writer.

My friend Haui Montaug also took his own life rather than endure late-phase AIDS. To think that they decided that suicide was the best of the choices open to them, still brings tears to my eyes as I write this.

So I created a performance, *A Certain Level of Denial*, that I framed as a mourning ritual. In the performance, I was lit only by slides of my paintings or by the slide projector. There was little humor and I would cry with each performance. At the end of the performance I'd walk off the stage holding a mound of black lace, a bodylike figure.

David Wojnarowicz died just before *A Certain Level of Denial* premiered at Lincoln Center, in the summer of 1992. I was standing on the loading dock at Lincoln Center after the premiere, waiting for Michael to arrive with the truck for my props, and I had a sort of fugue, a waking dream of David's death, which later became a part of the piece.

Losing David was particularly hard. He and I both lost our fathers to suicide and we both did political and sexual work and had similiar convictions. I felt closer artistically to him than to any other artist. Losing him was like losing the only other person who spoke my language.

The continued pressures of the NEA case and my friends' deaths put me deeper into depression. But we were all in a depression, a cultural depression.

HELLO MOTHER

Hello Mother,

Your son is dying. You knew—no, don't hang up. Your son is dying.

Hello gallery—SoHo—bullshit—

Hello art magazine cover crap,

Hello trendy East Villagers with rich parents—

Your friend, your artist is dying.

Where are you now?

Where are you now?

Hello ambulance,

Can you hear me? Today the I.V. of one of your clients came out and he was bleeding—yeah bleeding—all over, and you could give a shit. And as he was bleeding more and more, this ambulance didn't even know the way to the hospital.

Hello emergency room,

Don't bother helping someone sick. Don't bother helping someone dying. He's a leper. He's going to die anyway.

Hello admitting,

A patient is puking and bleeding in your mauve room.

Hey, there's no one to admit him. There's no one to admit him.

Hello hospital,

There's a patient who needs a wheelchair—but there ain't one. There's a patient who needs a blanket—but there ain't one. There's a patient caked in his own blood. Throw him a rag.

Hello society—
No answer.

Hello America—
No answer.

HE'S GOING HOME

He's going home. He's going home.
He's going home, you say.
We aren't having a goodbye party. We aren't having a last farewell. His leaving requires no gifts for us to buy.
Inside, we know this is no au revoir, no bon voyage. No get-well card.

It is a slow, uneven, painful passing.

Back to parents in Iowa.
Back to parents in Georgia.
Back to parents in Idaho.
Back to parents in Timbuktu.

No, we have never met your parents.
No, we have never met your Mom
            never been to the house where you grew up.

He's going home to drapes and homemade wine. To a room of cowboys and fire engines and twin beds. No one to share your bed ever again.

I can smell the maple bedposts, I can feel the chocolate-brown chenille bedspread. I can hear the clink-clank of the wire hangers with the name of the neighborhood dry cleaners printed on crinkly paper from years ago.

I can see the bathroom, papered yellow daffodils and a metal wastebasket that has rust stains on the bottom. I can see the china cabinet with your first palm-print clay ashtray. I can see the kitchen stove and the cake mixes. The TV—it still has the same shows on.

No more comfort.
Don't you realize that we don't want anything new?
Everything is changing so fast.

I don't want my parents to take care of me, he said.
I always wanted to take care of them, you said.

Sure, we will be visiting you in Idaho, Iowa, Georgia, Timbuktu.
Inside, we know we never will but pretending helps in times like these.
These are mean times. I can't explain what I mean or mean what I say. I don't know how to be there even though I'm there all the time.
This is the age of reverse.

After she was raped she took all of her paintings and underwear and clothing and sheets and burned them. She burned them in a garbage can in an alley, somewhere between Lunt and Greenleaf streets near the train, so she could scream as the train passed.

Please don't tell me that they are doing it to themselves. That you are doing it to yourself. Burning and looting. You realize that the only way that America responds is through violence. Through violence.

GIRL TALK

I got my purse but it ain't got any money—

    I make 63 cents to your dollar.

I got my make-up—

    Cause I got to hide who I am. You only want my words to come
out of a mouth that's kissable.

I got my perfume—

    A woman should keep her smells to herself.

I got my gloves—

I got my nylons on straight—

    A costume that keeps me in a position as flower, as animal.

I got my high heels—

    To have my walk shortened, to have my butt in the air so I'm like
    your pony like your porky

Call her a dog—

    Meaning you'll fuck her only if there is nothing else around.

Call her a cat—

    If she doesn't speak, just purrs when she's spoken to.

Call her a pussy—

    Her genitalia must be an animal's.

Call her a fox—

    When she knows how to wear her make-up.

Call her a cow—

    When she has had children and takes care of them well.

Call her a bitch—

    A female dog, concerned for her babies but not her man.

Call her a cold fish—

    When she doesn't want to get hurt and keeps her feelings to
    herself.

Call her a bird—Ladybird—

     Don't worry, she'll never be the President.

Call her a bull-dyke—

     Don't you get it? She doesn't need you.

call her a cat
if she doesn't speak
except purrs when spoken to

Last month he wanted to commit suicide but he didn't have the money for the gun. I called as soon as they had discovered the suicide note. Shock, grief, and despair. Even though he's served his country well they locked him up in a public hospital and he's treated like crap.

I'm so tired of well-meaning people.

When I walked into your room, the look on your face—
When I took your arm and led you down the stairs, there was blood everyplace.
When you walked in the hospital, you were left alone.

JESUS CHRIST, where are you now?

Cancer runs in some families—not in mine.
        We die too young.
Heart disease runs in some families—not in mine.
        Depression and mania
        Too-brief lives.

Some people think that I work too hard and do too much. But see, I can't sleep at nights—the terrors of the other side might be there. In my body sleeps the ghost of suicide
        of crazy
        of out of mind

I held her in my arms—
her positive tears soaked the sheets.
Even though she has money—
she'll be leaving soon.
She'll be leaving us soon.
Her children she will leave us.
Her children she will leave us.
Her children she will leave us.

WOMAN'S BEST FRIEND

LAST SUNDAY WE drove our rent-a-van down Sunset Boulevard to a yard sale. I was immediately attracted to the dozens of Spring-O-Lators in various pastels (stripper shoes). As I was squeezing my big foot into an eight-and-a-half I heard a scream and a piercing yelp, a sound I had never heard before. Behind me I saw the dog, young and grey and bearded, lying in the street, urine coming out of its holes. The owner, a young woman with hair the color of August prairies, was on the corner heaving in groans and pain and despair. I held the dog. Its eyes bobbed up and down in pain for ten seconds, and then it was over. I stroked the grey animal with her piss streaming down my toes, evaporating in the arid southwest air before it hit the curb.

Michael picked up the animal from the street and laid it to rest on the grass. At the same time, the driver who hit the dog returned to the scene in his over-sized, shiny black truck with raised tires, screaming, "That's what you get for not keeping your dog on a leash."

Yeah, you just killed the woman's dog, asshole! Now complete the job and make her feel guilty, terminally responsible. I hate people who must blame the victim, who have to have a reason to blame everything on somebody, like everyone is accountable for whatever happens to them—like karma. Karma was invented to keep the miserable in a position of acceptance.

The dog was covered with a yellow sheet, and the owner tried in vain to be adult and stay in control. She kept asking what she should do with the dog, twisting at the leash, but Sunset Boulevard is not a street of answers; it's a place of dreams.

Customers at the yard sale continued purchasing things and Michael kept telling the people that a good buy was not hiding under the sheet. But most bargain hunters wouldn't let a story about a dead dog stop them from peeking to make sure we weren't hiding some rare find.

The owner started to walk away. She began crossing the street in the same puppy fashion as her pet. I thought she looked like Mary Pickford. Shock does

different things to different people, and I didn't want anything to happen to her. I walked her to her apartment. She wasn't accepting kindness from strangers. I was merely an arm, a hand.

We approached her building. A woman was washing a 1970 Scamp on the street.

The woman let go of my hand and cried out, "Delly's dead! Delly's dead!" They embraced and held and held each other. And in their grief, they forgot the danger of two women lovers embracing. And within seconds, people in cars sneered as the two women were public with their sadness, held togeth-er in their devotion. Hostile, angry, remarks were made. "Perverts, kinks, ugly broads. If I was your man I'd force you both to enjoy cock."

I crept away. I wished I was bigger and could run after the meanies. But I was too slow, only human. Only a woman.

Michael and I stood watch by the shrouded pet. Soon the pair returned and carried the departed animal away among snickers and remarks from the cruel humans. "People like that shouldn't have a dog. Homosexuals shouldn't teach our children, and they shouldn't own pets."

Michael thought we should leave, but I had this overwhelming urge to buy this one orange sweater. There seemed to be so much past comfort in the sweater, with its wad of Kleenex in the pocket. I needed this sweater.

Later, as I tried on the sweater, I cleaned out the pockets. To my surprise, the Kleenex was covering a small maroon and ice-pink satin bag, tightly tied. Inside were keepsakes—a palmtree charm with a coconut made of a hot pink stone, a charm of the State of New York, earrings of crescent moons made of milky stone. There were six rings, one an emerald with pearls, another of thin garnets and diamonds, two of lucite and strange metals. Two wedding bands, probably her parents', dated 1911. Three gold coins dated 1858, 1861, and 1901. And in the bottom of the bag, rolled in yellow tissue, was a pin in the shape of a woman, with a sapphire in her hands highlighting her genitals. And a thick-banded gold ring. Both were inscribed in French and read

TO MY VIVIENNE WITH LOVE, ALWAYS, FLORENCE
1943

THE SESSION

MAN—Why don't you start with the beginning?

WOMAN—You mean Adam and Eve?

MAN—You said it, not me—

WOMAN—You asked me to start at the begining—Adam and Eve. Let's get it right. The snake was his dick, the apple his balls. So don't blame Eve.

MAN—What about God?

WOMAN—You should know better than me, because God is in your image. God is in your image. The image of man.

MAN—So you have a problem with God?

WOMAN—Yeah, you could say I got a problem with God. But I got my own gods, my own goddesses.

MAN—Tell me about your religious beliefs.

WOMAN—Well, first, I've got my fertility symbols. I got my Playtex bra, my support hose, my bunions from my three-inch spikes. Yeah, I wore those fertility heels to keep my job! I got my fertility bottle of peroxide and I have my nails long so I can claw at the devil.

MAN—So what you're saying is that you don't like being defined by your body, that you want other opportunities besides biological opportunities. Well, have you ever considered the imprisonment of the male and their role as daddy paycheck, as punisher, as provider?

WOMAN—Doctor, I hear some hostility in your tone. You feel imprisoned? Here's the apron strings now. You try to make the beds and make three meals a day for ten years and tell me about your gender liberation. I don't need to justify myself to you. You won't ever understand. You got the dick, the power, the hope. I could never grow up wishing to be president. All I can wish for is to be the president's lady and not get paid.

MAN—So you feel as if you've never existed in history.

WOMAN—Please don't look at me with your perverted sense of understanding. Please don't talk to me with your pathetic overshaved sensitivity,

because you make me more determined than ever that there is nothing worse than a liberal shrink.

MAN—You're just angry because you never had a career.

WOMAN—Here's my resume—I have had three children, two miscarriages, and one abortion. I've been a mother, a whore, and a slave. I've been needed, rejected, never valued.

MAN—How's your drinking?

WOMAN—You don't get it, do you? You see Kitty Dukakis, you see Betty Ford drunk and drugged. Why? Because they're bored. BOREDOM. The carpool just didn't do it. The ironing board as an artform just didn't make it. [Pause.] Say something! SAY SOMETHING!

MAN—What do you want me to say?

WOMAN—This whole setup is that I've got something wrong and you've got something right. But I don't see it that way—You got something wrong and I got something right.

MAN—Tell me what's wrong with me.

WOMAN—Well Doctor, you get very uncomfortable around competitive sports. You especially feel uncomfortable around football. You try to say it's because you are a sensitive male, but it's probably because you were ridiculed for not being athletic. There were perhaps beatings, not severe, but one of them gave you an erection. You fantasize about being with an older woman with fleshy, sagging breasts and skin that has been wrinkled by the sun wearing a tight red cocktail dress. I'm shaking you up, aren't I?

MAN—Actually, I was never beaten, I was neglected. My father suffered from Parkinson's disease—

WOMAN—Oh, your father was castrated by his illness. You never wanted to play sports because you didn't want to appear stronger than your father.

MAN—Let's look at your life. You are soon to be divorced. You have a lot of problems ahead. Raising a family alone. I assume you will want a job. Let's get on with your life. Since women don't play an important part in the world—let's be more pragmatic, realistic. Let's not discuss religious, political, or sexual issues. Let's just concentrate on your management talents, good old ways and means.

WOMAN—Have you ever had a dog that crawled in the corner whenever the broom came out? That dog was beaten by that broom and even though you treat the dog with love and respect, the dog will still cower in the corner and will cry and yelp. I'm that dog.

MAN—When you think of a broom do you think of an erect penis?

WOMAN—Just remember one thing—a man might have his dick, but a woman has her feminine instinct.

MAN—You aren't wearing a bra today, are you?

WOMAN—No, I'm not wearing a bra today. In fact, I'm not wearing anything today.

MAN—You had a choice in your appearance—you don't have to wear make-up or a skirt or perfume. By not wearing a bra, by being naked, you are saying that you desire me, you want me!

WOMAN—Let me say this: women are tired of defending and explaining their bodies, the care of their bodies, the presentation of their bodies. Women are tired of being looked at as a loaded gun.

MAN—Tell me about your sexual fantasies. I'd like to know if you fantasize about being raped. If you've had sex with animals.

WOMAN—Gee, Doc, what do you do in your spare time?

AUNT ENID

AUNT ENID HAD been patiently waiting for us to visit for at least ten years. That's when she had been given a bottle of 40-year-old scotch, which she finally opened upon our arrival. The scotch had been given to her wrapped in a beautiful gold-foiled box, and she had always featherdusted the container with attention.

Aunt Enid did not know exactly who she was waiting for, but she always felt that she would know them when she saw them. Her life was one in which she was constantly seeing people suffer. Her sister Lilly was left to die by her brother-in-law, Lou, who didn't believe in doctors, except for himself. When Lilly gave birth to twin girls, Lou was mad because twin boys would have brought home better paychecks.

It was then that Enid had a yearning, an uncanny feeling that came between her ribs, her gut, and her heart. It was a feeling that swam inside her.

When Lilly died, Enid held her in her arms. She cut pieces of her dead sister's nightgown and bedclothes. What Enid began that night was the Suffering Quilt. It was made from the clothing and linens of people who had suffered unnecessarily. She would embroider names, stories, and emblems on each patch. After that night, Enid never returned to church.

It came by coincidence, our visit to Enid's. She was waiting for us because she knew that eventually someone would arrive who would appreciate the suffering quilt. She had last showed it some fifteen years before, to her women's group, but the viewing was dismissed as some madcap folly. Enid realized that neither family nor friends would ever appreciate the art, and so she would have to find a different way of communicating.

Enid's first thought was to use nature. She would gather turquoise sequins and throw them to the wind. She walked up Superstition Mountain and threw the sequins into the air. Then she began to feed the birds with a special rosemary-toasted bread. These were like her quilt—small gestures that made the world better.

Enid started going to the library and looking in old phone directories for names and street addresses she liked. She would write, "It's the small things in life that matter." She was going through a 1959 directory from Chicago, Ill., when she came upon Devoted Heart, 777 Bittersweet Place.

Enid took off her gloves. She knew that this was the person to see her quilt. She wrote down the address in her notebook and placed it in her purse that had a tapestry image of Montmartre, Paris woven on its front. Her first message to Devoted Heart would be simple but substantial. It would be a list of the towns and villages along Interstate 80 in Pennsylvania.

Bellefonte

Woodland

Snow Shoe

Altoona

Lock Haven

Lamar

Lazanton

Mile Run

Mountaintop

Marshall's Creek

Lightstreet

Milford

Dubois

Clarion

Mercer

Buckhorn

Bloomsburg

Shawnee

Hickory Run

Scrubgrass

White Deer

and Lake Harmony.

ROADKILL

SHE COULDN'T DRIVE by car anymore. It wasn't the cost of oil, it wasn't the driving, it was roadkill.

As a child, she was told to stop crying when the car ran into the doe. The mother was crossing the road with her new fawn.

Spindly legs and all.

Baseball was on. A homerun score. No one heard my cries when I saw the mother and child in the road. Later Daddy said, "Dead fox—just outside of Milton, approaching Bloomsburg."

Said, "Wish it was a man deer we hit. Wish it was a buck. Then we'd have us some horns." From that, I learned my first lesson in economics. Even a dead male is worth something.

When our car hit the mother, her hind leg was torn off immediately. For a moment that leg stayed at the window of the passenger side, with the blood and warm flesh stuck to the window. Never liked anything warm and wet from then on. Funny how memories are.

Later that same year it happened all over again. I can't remember why we were in our car. I had my dolly, though. I remember seeing the massive doe and how impressive she was. She was running along the thicket. Then I screamed, for her child had bolted out into the road. It was too late. Too quick. My daddy always drove with a heavy foot. The young body crushed against the windshield. Even though it was small, it still blocked my father's view. The mother called from behind and charged the car. My father stopped and pushed the deer-child off the window. With that, the mother charged at us again, rammed her entire strength into us. The head coming right into me, right at me. The doe wouldn't stop. She had nothing to live for, we had killed her child. And I looked at my dolly and knew we did wrong.

My father reached into the glove compartment and took out a 45. He told me to get down. He fired the gun over and over and over again, too many times.

A deer should only die once.

But it was such a little gun, my father would later explain.

Daddy put the gun back into the glove compartment and muttered "They're not even worth getting out of the car for. Buzzards will be here before long. Wish it been a buck 'cause mercy, we'd have some horn. Only a woman and her child, probably a female child, it was so slow. Only a female, a mother could get herself killed that way."

And when we returned home on the same road, my daddy tried to teach me something by saying, "Animals don't have feelings, they have instinct." We passed the child deer who had dragged its body toward its momma.

And I cried "Daddy, let's help them. They're alive!"

Daddy said "Don't worry, they'll be dead in a few minutes."

Then he drove right over them both.

IT'S MY BODY

LAST NIGHT I heard crying—it was a piercing cry—and I awoke, and in my room were hundreds and hundreds of women. And they were all crying, all weeping, all marching.

I saw the Virgin Mary and she carried a sign that read "PRO-CHOICE." I saw Cleopatra and she wore a T-shirt that read, "VAGINAL PRIDE." I saw Joan of Arc and she wore a button that said, "THE POPE IS SATAN." I saw Josephine Baker and she held a sign that read, "U.S. OUT OF MY UTERUS."

And then I saw my Aunt Mandy and she was screaming. She came up to me and I said, "I'm sorry that you died from cancer of the uterus," and she said, "Child, I died of an illegal abortion at fifty with this damn gag in my throat. When you die like I died, they don't even let you scream. Bled to death, I did. Rats ate my insides out. I was fifty."

Then I saw the ghost of my childhood friend, Pam, who died by her own hands. She just didn't have the money to go to New York City, where abortion was legal in 1973. She didn't have the money. So one day she opened a can of Drano and poured it into her. She thought she could just burn it out. But she was only twelve. She was only twelve.

Let me tell you about children dying. Let me tell you about the sanctity of life. The infant mortality rate in Harlem is higher than it is in some Third World countries.

The Far Right wants women to obey a Patriarchal Disorder. Well we women aren't going back to our only choice is to clean up after men.

Our choice is a woman becoming President. A woman becoming Pope. Whether these male control freaks like it or not, we're going to feminize this planet. Baby, we're going to show them HYSTERIA, we're going to show them OUT OF CONTROL, CRAZY, HELL-BENT, OVER-EMOTIONAL, PMSed, IRRATIONAL WOMEN united in rage to overturn this male control of our lives.

No one is controlling me.

Say it, sister.

NO ONE IS CONTROLLING MY BODY.

We've been raped.

We've been discriminated against.

We've been oppressed.

We've been persecuted.

We've been controlled.

MEN ARE NOT CONTROLLING US ANY LONGER.

And the spirits of women are remembering when men would gag women as they performed their hatchet jobs, and the men would say, "I'll kill you if you scream."

But this time we're screaming.

This time we're screaming.

TESTIMONY OF THE REALITY
THAT LIFE IS UNFAIR AND UNJUST

I HAD JUST given my last dollar away when the barefoot young woman approached me for money. She was pregnant, filthy, with sores all over her body, smelly and sick. It was rush hour and hundreds of people walked by her with their visible screens of protection. I walked by her, and it hit me—the despair in our society, our culture, our city, and that despair hit my belly and I cramped into sickness. All the grief of wandering souls just became too much. My shield down, puking to other homeless souls.

I am this culture. I am this sickness. I don't want to leave my house no more.

Someone is talking to me again. But all that is on my mind are the results of my HIV Test.

Someone is talking to me again. But all I'm thinking about is my friend having his feeding tube removed.

Someone is talking to me again. But all I'm thinking about is the family living in the bus stop on Sunset Boulevard.

I look at your face. Broken and bleeding and pus in your eyes. "Sorry, man. Money went to baby in dead woman's soul. No kidding."   Fifty dollars means nothing in this town.

I feel like I'm fighting a war. (You are.)

I feel like I'm fighting a war.

I've been poor, but not as poor as you are now.

I've been dead, but not as dead as you are now.

Take my money.

Take my soul.

It isn't worth it, to live being witness to this suffering.

SOMETIMES I JUST CAN'T MOVE, WAITING FOR THE DRAGON TO STOP BREATHING ITS FIRE.

ACCEPTING THAT MAYBE THAT DRAGON WON'T EVER GO AWAY.

I feel nothing but impending doom, for I live in a society that has rules for certain standards of behavior. I wish I could live in a society where two people of the same sex could openly kiss and show affection. I wish I lived in a society where gays and lesbians could adopt children without the look in your liberal face that says you still believe I'm a pervert.

I go into your liberal home, your college town, your *Vanity Fair* existence of brie and blush chablis, but you don't trust me with your children. You don't trust me.

I am only an accessory to your surface life.

To invite to parties.

I see how you always have paper cups and plates ready for me when I enter your home. I know the real reason why, after I used your restroom, the rest of the family always used the one upstairs.

And of course I noticed, when I spent the night at my sister's, the professor of human resources, when I visit my brother, the doctor, they remove toothbrushes and shavers from the bathrooms.

And you never let my nieces or nephews come visit. But after a few too many drinks, your mask slips more, and you say, "I know you'll understand, but we don't want our children to be attracted to your influences." What you are saying is, you don't want your children growing up to be—

A QUEER

A FAIRY

A DYKE

A PERSON WITH A LISP

A QUEEN, A POOFTER

A BUTCH DYKE LESBO

I hate white, protected liberalism and its safe, covered, homophobic, putrid ways.

SOMETIMES I JUST CAN'T MOVE, WAITING FOR THE DRAGON TO STOP BREATHING ITS FIRE.

ACCEPTING THAT MAYBE THAT DRAGON WON'T EVER GO AWAY.

I walk through this town and I just see everything as a disease. I see cars as giant carcasses in deserts of lice. I see buildings as sharks sucking in the sky so I suffocate. That's what living is about for me. That's what trying to survive means to me.

So don't tell me about your boring heterosexual problems

Your legal weddings that I'm denied.

Your divorces that I'm denied.

Showing displays of public affection to the person you love.

Going to the church that excommunicated me.

And in the next bite of tofu and alfalfa sprouts, you talk about your hair color or staying on your diet.

Sometimes, I pretend those are my problems.

Because this week three of my friends have died.

And when I told you in my hushed voice—for uttering their names was that painful—your idea of comfort was, "It shouldn't hurt that much. You knew they were going to die."

"It must get easier to mourn with the more that die."

"Who's going to take their apartment?"

Yeah, he's dead.

"Oh, that's too bad, so many are going," you say, without looking into my eyes. Business-as-usual and the-show-must-go-on are bitter songs to my ears.

Yeah, he's dead. There's no one to bury him. He's getting a paupers' grave. He's dead. No family. No mother. No father. No sister. No brother to accept him as god's creature.

SOMETIMES I JUST CAN'T MOVE, WAITING FOR THE DRAGON TO STOP BREATHING ITS FIRE.

ACCEPTING THAT MAYBE THAT DRAGON WON'T EVER GO AWAY.

LOST HOPE

YESTERDAY I CALLED to say goodbye to my friend. He had AIDS and had decided to take his own life.

That's right—my friend has AIDS and I think he took his own life last night.

Let me say it again.

My friend lost 45 pounds last month, and last night I think he took his own life.

Let me say this again.

My friend had no reason to live but he had a reason to die. He couldn't control the suffering. He couldn't control the anger. He couldn't control the depression. He couldn't control the government. He couldn't control the hatred. He couldn't control this country. He couldn't. But he could control his death.

He couldn't kill Helms but he could kill himself.

AIDS wouldn't kill him—he'd kill AIDS.

He didn't want to die like Rock Hudson—he'd rather live like Sylvia Plath.

Today, I pick up the phone, but I just can't call to see if he did it. I said to him, "Please, please let me see you one more time." I'm here in Chicago. I can't call to see if he did it—if he got the Seconal. I haven't called to see if he got the Seconal, ground it up, and shot it up.

Or maybe he used a gun.

Or maybe he used a knife.

No, my friend is not a violent man.

You see, I don't want to be here. I want to be on East 2nd St. and Bowery, pleading with my friend not to take his life. But he is so weak he cannot speak. He can only feel. He can only think. It's like the way I pleaded with the world to save my Daddy. Like the way I should have pleaded with Ethyl when he sliced his own wrists and then bled to death in the hot bathwater.

But I didn't see the signs. Although I'm always privileged with being given signs—and hindsight.

I don't want to be here. I want to be with my friend—when everyone was healthy, when we all had dreams, when we all had destinies. Suicide is not such a great way to die.

Yeah, I'll tell you about art. Yeah, I'll tell you about performance art. Yeah, Ethyl had AIDS.

Let's make some blood prints off of Ethyl's wrists. Let's take some photos of my friend killing himself—blow up the photo—and put some God dam text on it that says, DEAD—and make an edition of 10.

Yeah, let me tell you about art.

You see, today I found myself in Edgewater, standing in the same spot where 2 Chicago pigs followed me out of a bar when I was 21. And just as I got to Bryn Mawr and Broadway, they stopped my car and told me that I was speeding (which I wasn't), told me I was drunk (which I wasn't). Then they said they could straighten everything out if we went to Thorndale Beach and did some hanky-panky. I'm not going to tell you what happened next—but I don't like the color blue.

Baby, I don't need no videotape—I got my own memories.

Today I hear that it's donut day in Chicago. I get a fear up me when I hear "Donuts," cause when I hear "Donuts" all I think of are Chicago cops eating donuts and doing nothing while I'm attacked by 15 youths. When I screamed to the police for help from across the street, they threw me a donut and said, "That's what a girl gets when she comes out at night."

I don't need no videotape—I got my own memories.

I'm in Rogers Park, standing outside the door where my ex-boyfriend parked for days. One day I let him in by mistake. Later, when I reported to the police that my ex-boyfriend had raped me after I let him in, Policeman said, "Doesn't sound like a crime to me or we'd have to arrest every man in sight."

I don't need no videotape—I got my own memories.

My friend says he's going to take his own life because he wants me to remember him well, not sick. He says he's had a good life. He says, "Karen, if I have my way, I'm going to be coming back in a more evolved state."

AN ACT OF CONSCIENCE

"I CANNOT BE effective. I cannot change this world," she said.
"If I cannot even clean my room, how can I change the world?"

Last nite, you died again for me.
There was nothing to live for.
I see your last performance all too clearly
On an island inhabited by souls of grey and prejudice
You were always the other
To your parents. They never acknowledged your true real self.
They tolerated
They left you to God.
We all knew you were great.
We all held you as our monarch.
There was nothing to live for—
But there was something to die for.

AIDS wouldn't kill you
You'd kill AIDS

And that final voyage
of your body floating in its own blood
Arms sliced at wrists
The tainted blood flowing out of our genius.
When you say, "He had no other choice"—
I pray for your soul.

Suicide is not such a nice way to die.
Suicide is a big price to pay
I keep thinking, for I need to drown out the sound of your flesh cut.

I keep on saying "It's alright," because if we don't

we are all doomed.

We must accept that this world is cruel.

What killed you

was not accepting the homosexual

as natural and good

You were always looked at as deviant

perverted, bad, bringer of disease

And one learns to live in a world that makes you a deviant,

an untouchable

so you become invisible

not to get in the way

THEY'LL JUST BEAT THE QUEER OUT OF YOU

and if you come out

They'll deny you work—That'll get the queer out of you

They'll deny you legal rights—That'll shake the queer out of you

They'll deny you a civil marriage—You'll never legally be a couple.

Your love is never quite good enough.

That'll depress the queer out of you.

They'll deny you recognition, force the mask, the costume

So you can never speak freely your feelings.

That'll destroy your queer heart

But what does it matter?

We've been taught that queers don't have hearts. They live only for sexual

deviance.

And after you died—

I relive all of my friends' deaths

over and over and over again

til it's all one big death.

And I remember when you sent me

the amarylis

A flower that grows without water
The flowers you send me
the poems you write me
the stories you told me of Pekin, Ill.
secrets I'll never tell
But when you told me that I was your sunshine—
I always looked at you as a brighter star
But I never knew you felt the darkness
in your poems—
When I saw you
you were always the ACTOR
But what could I say
when I asked what's wrong
in a letter you said
60 FRIENDS DEAD

We all knew how it affected you
for it affects us
But you always made us forget on stage
You always came to me in letters
I made you remember
Except I ignored the signs
I should have been better
but you're such a clever man
an actor
as good as my daddy.
You both made me feel.
So even though you wrote me signs
I still didn't know what to say to
60 FRIENDS DEAD, KAREN.

Even though I'm the daughter of a murderer
the sister of a mania

the child of depression—

even though there is death on my hands

even though I believe in life after death—

my crime is that I have courage

and I tried to give you HOPE

when I knew you lived DESPAIR

I should have let you

cry those million tears.

But the clown never cries

The man is the woman

The actor denies his own script

I wish I could have showed you tears.

You didn't need to be so strong.

FALL APART

FALL APART

FALL APART at the seams

But instead you sliced your own wrists.

Yes, you can be effective.

Yes, you can change the world.

And when you feel you don't have the strength, you don't want to get involved,

that it is easier to be quiet—that it is easier just to slip by—

You just think of Ethyl's wrists.

You just think of too-brief lives.

You just count them in your mind. There aren't enough fingers on your hands.

And you just sit back in your own comforts

And you wait it out

You just count your money

and count your dead friends

You just wait it out.

IN MEMORY OF

I WAKE UP in the middle of the night—I'm sure I haven't slept—and I turn on the light and I take out my old phone books and I start going through them. I go through all of the old names. Then I take out my Rolodex and I start with the A's and I go through, stopping at my friend's names, my deceased friends' names, my dead friends' names. I JUST CAN'T TAKE THEM OUT. I just can't take them out and throw their names in the trash.

Sometimes I pick up the phone and it's 3:00 A.M. I dial the number and I ask for them by name.

Sometimes the phone just rings.

Disconnected.

A new person speaks.

Sometimes I pretend to talk to my dead friends on the phone—as if the phone was ringing in heaven.

Sometimes I leave the Rolodex open at your phone number, because   for a moment I forget—

There is no ritual that makes me feel any better.

Praying just doesn't do it.

Praying just doesn't work for me.

Working just doesn't make me forget

The Higher Power never shows up.

Letting go doesn't work, because I ain't got nothing to hold on to.

I want to hold on to you.

Crying helps.

Crying helps.

It's best at night, when I can't watch TV anymore. When the streets are silent except for the paper trucks with tomorrow's news. The clock ticks and the tears swell up.

> I'll light you a candle.

I'll say you a prayer.

Baby, we're past hope

        past hope

        past hope

Sometimes I dream that you're alive and that everything is fine and that we're all eating big meals with lots of almond-and-raisin stuffing but then I cry, because it's only a dream

        only a dream

        only a dream

Sometimes I make beautiful paintings with your name hidden in the design.
Sometimes I embroider your name on the soles of my socks and on   my hankerchiefs—but that seems like another century.

I remember when you told me you were ill. Not just a cold. Not just the flu. We drank 2 bottles of wine. Somehow we didn't get drunk. We wanted to, but we didn't.
He knew it was the last time I'd see him. The last time he'd see me.
We'd never see Paris together.
We'd never make our film together.
We'd never tell each other secrets again.
I wouldn't be there for him anymore.
He couldn't be there for me anymore.
All those experiences lost somehow.
But we can dream.

        I dream

        I dream.

Of a time when life was full of promises of growing old.
Then I just cry myself to sleep, whispering,

    Oh, Johnny,

    Oh, Johnny, Johnny I miss you.

AUNT ENID 2

DEVOTED HEART RECEIVED the letter from Aunt Enid. She took everything into consideration. Devoted Heart had failing health, the kind that doesn't get worse—it just shows that your body doesn't work anymore.

Devoted noticed 3 things:

1) That day, birds began nesting on her porch. Bluejays and wrens, who are normally enemies, were getting along now.
2) A man on line next to her at the Post Office was born in the same small town, Janesville, WI, as her father.
3) She craved the smell of lavender and newborn puppies.

Devoted Heart read the list of towns insightfully and only one town affected her in an emotional way—it was Bloomsburg, just outside of Milton, where her father had hit a deer when she was a little girl. Devoted Heart went to her safety deposit box and took out $25.00 and she placed a personal ad in the Bloomsburg newspaper. The ad read as follows:

> READ TOWNS WITH INTEREST
> OPEN TO ALL SUGGESTIONS
> —DEVOTED HEART

Aunt Enid saw the ad while she was in the laundromat. She knew that this was the sign she had been waiting for. She mailed the quilt to Devoted Heart, 1st Class, wrapped in lavender tissue. The box was from a clothing store in Janesville, WI.

When Devoted Heart received the package from the Post Office her heart jumped a beat. She carried it to the porch. It was a spring afternoon, a Wednesday at 3:30, to be exact, and Devoted sat on her porch examining the quilt. She put her hand on the fabrics and felt all the lives. Devoted cried and cried right there on the porch in her rocking chair and fell asleep with the blanket on her. Only she never woke again.

The birds flew down to Devoted and sat on her body. They began taking apart the quilt thread by thread to make their nests. This spring was a happy spring, for the nesting birds had homes of flannel and silk and wool for their eggs to hatch in.

And here the story ends except for one last note—from Aunt Enid. Clutched in Devoted Heart's hand were the words:

SMALL GESTURES THAT MAKE THE WORLD BETTER

EPILOGUE

LAST NIGHT I dreamed that a huge skyscraper crashed, collapsed. It was filled with artists and art from all continents, from all cultures all over the world. It was a U.N. of creativity, of expression. Every artist had been given a plot on which to create a work of art. Now, I associate, and I see that every artist had been given a grave on which to create a work of art. Then the building came tumbling down, and that skyscraper was you. That skyscraper was you.

Somewhere here is a message.
Somewhere here is a metaphor.
Somewhere here is a cosmic web that makes sense of a terrible time.
I stay up nights contemplating this.
But nothing ever comes of it.

* * *

OLLIE NORTH AND other right-wing politicians were using my name in their fundraising letters. One day in Nyack I picked up the local Catholic church's Sunday bulletin, and there was a diatribe against me. Rush Limbaugh talked about me frequently on his show. The feeling of going to church, or getting into a cab in a distant town, and seeing or hearing yourself being condemned, is difficult to take.

Limbaugh said that I had sex and masturbated on stage, that I used real feces in my work. I eventually had to take legal action to put him on notice that what he was saying about me was untrue, and that, if he persisted in saying such things, it could legally be considered "with malice" and slanderous. He shut up.

They say that there's no such thing as bad publicity, but this publicity was having a negative effect on my livelihood. Throughout this period, I had protests, picketers, threats, assaults, obscene and violent mail and phone calls, city and state inquiries made into my appearances, cancellations. . . . I never left the house without my attorneys' phone numbers. And I called them often.

What I discovered is that public support is difficult to escape. All around us, there is government support in some form. Whether it is the US Post Office, liquor licenses, the FCC, city-owned buildings—you find public support everywhere, and everywhere you find it, the government can try to use it to control people. So the issue is more than the NEA. There are many more ways to silence speech that some find offensive.

In order to book me, any venue or institution would have to be prepared to deal with the controversy that always seemed to follow in my wake. That was a lot to ask of anyone. And I was being given more exposure in the press than other artists—whether it was because chocolate is titillating, because I was straight and the press is homophobic, or just because it was my name in the title of the court case, I don't know.

Michael and I had decided to have a baby, and at that point, in early 1992, I was several months pregnant. I started spotting, but I had a show in Madison, Wisconsin. I never made the performance. I had a miscarriage. I still remember the doctor asking me if I was "under any stress."

IN SPRING 1991, I was asked by British curators John Bewley and Simon Hubert to participate in a festival in Newcastle, England with the members of the NEA 4 and other censored artists, including Annie Sprinkle. I decided to create an installation that included volunteer performers.

MOMENTO MORI

15

I went to England that fall. I was given a space above a night club, in an empty old warehouse with no heat. On the walls, I painted the texts that would later become "A Certain Level of Denial." My idea was to take public sculpture one step further. This sculpture would be created by the public, as they interacted with the installation.

The installation, which centered around grieving rituals, was called *Momento Mori*. The first ritual was the "Ribbon Gate." Visitors entering the installation were met by a guide, who stood at an ornate iron gate. Everyone would select a ribbon from a basket, and would tie the ribbon to the gate in memory of someone who had died of AIDS. As the piece progressed, the gate became more and more thickly covered with ribbons.

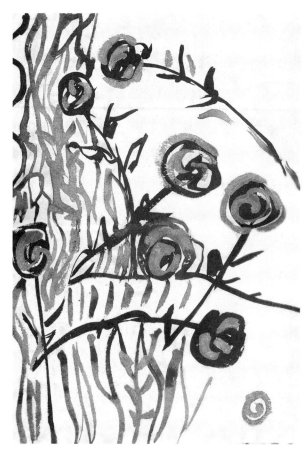

The second ritual was "The Carnation Wall." A wall of white lace hung from the ceiling. Each visitor was invited by a guide to place a red carnation in the lace in memory of those who had died of AIDS. As the lace got full and the flowers dried, the Wall, from far away, came to resemble an abstract painting. I would add another layer of lace when the first layer became full.

Momento Mori also included a row of beds, each with a nightstand, bedclothes, and a chair. Here the painting was actually the memory—the memory conjured in the viewer's mind. Not everyone has a loved one who has died of AIDS, but the image of the bedside vigil for the loved one who is sick is like a cultural memory that everyone shares.

MICHAEL OVERN

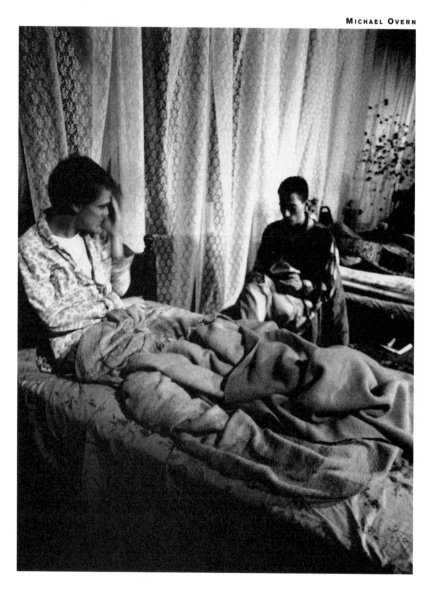

A DIFFERENT KIND OF INTIMACY

Performers sat in the beds, representing patients or sick people. Viewers could sit next to the bed, in the position of friend, family member, or caregiver. People were very moved by the piece.

After Newcastle, *Momento Mori* went to the Kitchen, and then the curator Julie Lazar brought it to the Museum of Contemporary Art in Los Angeles. In L.A. there were 12 to 15,000 ribbons tied to the gate and four hundred people volunteered to perform in the sickbeds. Many of the people who volunteered were mourning the loss of a loved one themselves.

The installation in L.A. also included an antique chest filled with sand. Viewers were invited to write the name of someone who had died of AIDS in the sand. Then they were asked to erase the name back into the sand. Parents, lovers, friends, families, and children of those who had died came to participate.

Later, I expanded on this part of the piece. In September 1993, at Hallwalls in Buffalo, I filled a large room with sand. The mound of sand formed itself into valleys and hills and I covered it with candles. The walls of the room were painted gold. Here, as with the chest, people were invited to enter the room and write the names of those they had lost to AIDS.

MICHAEL OVERN

Lighting —

Lighting is to be low. One light in the sand, in the chest. Light is not be in ~~[illegible]~~ eyes of person performing ritual.

A cloth is provided so that you can cover the table or pedestal with. If part of the table shows and it is annoying paint black.

Ritual

public writes the name or names of those they have loved and lost to Aids.

If you need any other instructions please call.

Thankyou. Hope all goes well.

Karen Finley

After performing the ritual, I realized, people needed a place to sit quietly for a while to transition back into their everyday worlds. So at Gallery 76 at the Ontario College of Art in Toronto I made a companion installation, the "Vacant Chair." The installation consisted of a plain wooden chair covered, adorned with flowers, next to a child's chair. The vacant chair represented the presence of the deceased person. When a person dies, we feel their presence in their absence — the vacant place at the table, the vacant space in the bed, the empty space in the closet, the vacant chair.

AFTER THE NEA controversy began, I had received a letter from Louise Bourgeois asking me to accept an award on her behalf in Washington DC. The award was being given by *Sculpture* magazine; it was for Louise's life's work and her contributions to sculpture. I met with Louise, who was then 80, to discuss what she wanted me to speak about. She wanted me to talk about my experiences with censorship and my views as a female artist. She told me how, as a young sculptor, the male sculptors of her generation were recognized way before she was. It was not until she was 55 that she began selling work.

Around the same time, I had an exhibition of my drawings at a gallery in East Hampton. On the day of the opening of the show, Hannah Wilke came to the gallery to meet me. She was suffering from cancer and she would not live out the year. She sat down and said, "Everything you are doing I did before you. But I was not noticed or given the recognition that you are given." Hannah did not say this with bitterness. She said it with an objective, third-person approach to history: she was born; and then I was born after her. I benefited from her struggles as she benefited from the struggles of the women before her. She wanted me to be aware of this ongoing lineage. She felt it was important for me to recognize this passage.

She also told me that what was causing her cancer was experiencing her mother's cancer, and the way Claes had treated her, which she had internalized. She was referring to Claes Oldenberg, her lover. A few years later, my friend Dino Mauritus and his boyfriend Patrick Moore bought a Claes Oldenberg lithograph at an AIDS benefit. When I saw it, I was in shock, for the image was a woman who resembled Hannah, hanging from a meat hook. It was eerie because of what Hannah had told me. On the glass beside the image, I scrawled the things in red grease marker that she had told me about Claes.

Momento Mori had a companion installation, "Women's Room," which dealt with some of the issues that encounters like these had raised for me. The installation included a series of vanities with text written on the mirrors in red paint that looked like lipstick. "I was not created to please men." "I was not expected to be talented." The vanities were decorated fetishistically with hats, jewelry, and other items. Near the vanities, a nude woman lay on a bed surrounded by dead birds. I hand-painted a text, "It's My Body," on the walls surrounding her.

MICHAEL OVERN

The participatory element of "Women's Room" was the "Mother's Maiden Name Wall." Here, viewers were invited to write their mother's maiden names directly onto the wall. There were colored pencils and markers available. The names were written over each other and they formed a beautiful abstract wall drawing.

A producer from the *Dennis Miller Show* saw my installation and asked me to be a guest on the show and to perform "It's My Body." Michael and I thought that the text would be problematic for television since it included scathing references to the Pope, Cardinal O'Connor, and President Bush. But we figured they knew what they were getting into, so I went ahead and went on the show.

There was a rehearsal. I performed my piece without incident: the audience seemed ok with the material and I heard nothing from the producers. But when I performed the piece during the actual taping of the show, the audience seemed a bit in shock.

After performing, I went to sit with Dennis on the set and he didn't give me a chance to speak. He kept talking about freedom of expression, and he looked very nervous. As soon as the taping was over, there was a discussion behind closed doors, and, to make a long story short, I wound up on the cutting room floor. It seemed so hypocritical, because Dennis Miller tries to be so political, so cutting-edge, and instead he was acting like Ed Sullivan forcing Mick Jagger to sing "Let's Spend Some Time Together" instead of "Let's Spend the Night Together." It's fine to have Henry Rollins looking so punk rock but not really talking about anything other than nice, safe liberal politics. But no pro-choice polemics, please—no female politics. If Dennis really wanted to be cutting-edge, he would have let the segment run even though it did deal with an incendiary topic. Instead, he replaced me with a comedian who made jokes about women.

ICHAEL AND I started retreating to Provincetown in the early 1990s. We would vacation there—bring our parents, and relax. I felt comfortable on the Cape and in a town that was pro-queer. I liked being where people of the same sex could show affection to each other without the fear of retribution.

16

ENOUGH IS ENOUGH

(Although, later on, I had a censorship battle over performing my piece *American Chestnut* in Provincetown.)

Being in Provincetown gave me peace, and it also brought my sense of humor back. One day Michael and I wandered into a 12-step program gift shop. Everything—T-shirts, mugs—had a 12-step theme. It made me think of one time when I was performing in Boulder and I went on a radio show, and the host said that she thought I should forgive Jesse Helms. I responded, "I don't believe in forgiving someone who has practically ruined my life." I never understood the reasoning behind forgiving someone who is actively trying to make your life miserable.

I decided then and there to write my own self-help book. Writing this parody allowed the humor to come back into my work. *Enough is Enough* came out in the fall of 1993, just after my daughter, Violet, was born.

from *Enough is Enough*

WHY LET GO WHEN
YOU CAN CONTROL?

BEING IN CONTROL

Most people will advise you to let go and go with the flow. I ask, why? I advise you to be in control of as many people, situations and lives as possible. The most important reason to be in control is that it creates a much more interesting and complex life. And having a complex life is where it's at, especially if you are ever going to sell your life story. Being a control freak means you call the shots all the time.

Usually the people who tell us to stop controlling others are the ones who are in control of something but want to appear to be free, easy and open. Getting people not to be in control changes the power structure. It creates a bunch of selfless, uncomplaining goody-two-shoes to take over and dominate. We are told to try and stop controlling others, but the reason we don't stop is because this is all we've got.

So stop the crap about trying to stop controlling others' lives. If all else fails, it's always good to pick a family member or friend whose behavior you want to control. You never will change their behavior, but it's your duty to try and control a family member. If you didn't, you wouldn't visit them at all. Then what would you do with your time? That goes for trying to control family gatherings—you know you won't, but you try to anyway, just for the hell of it. Controlling spouses is good too. We never do control them, but it sure is worth it to try.

It's important to get stressed out by having to be in control. Hopefully everyone will need you and your valuable time. Then you will deserve a vacation. Remember, being in control all the time makes vacations more important. The only control no-no is: Don't be a weekend control freak or vacation control freak.

MOTTO:

Why let go when you can control?

I BLAME MY MOM AND MY
GREAT GRANDFATHER - I
BLAME THE QUEST OF THE
HOLY GRAIL AND THE INVENTION
OF THE AUTOMOBILE. I BLAME
MY DAD AND
THE WAY HE
SPRINKLED
SUGAR. I
BLAME THE
WEATHER. I
BLAME televi-
SION FOR
EVERYTHING.
I BLAME ALL OF THESE
THINGS ON WHY I AM
SUCH A Profound INDIVIDUAL.

BLAME

The best way to make our lives easier is to blame someone else for our mistakes. We know when we have made a mistake, so why the hell should we need to suffer the humiliation of accepting it publicly? It wastes time.

Blaming relatives is the best. Kids should blame parents for why they are so messed up, and parents should blame their kids for why they haven't done what they wanted with their lives. But then blaming transportation, the mail and the system also works to deflect the blame from yourself.

When you aren't to blame: then is the time to blame yourself. People will say, "No, no, you aren't to blame." Then cry and squeak a little and everyone will think you are so wonderful to accept blame for something you aren't responsible for.

Tip:

Blaming others for your mistakes is an effective way of getting out of a big mess.

Lie

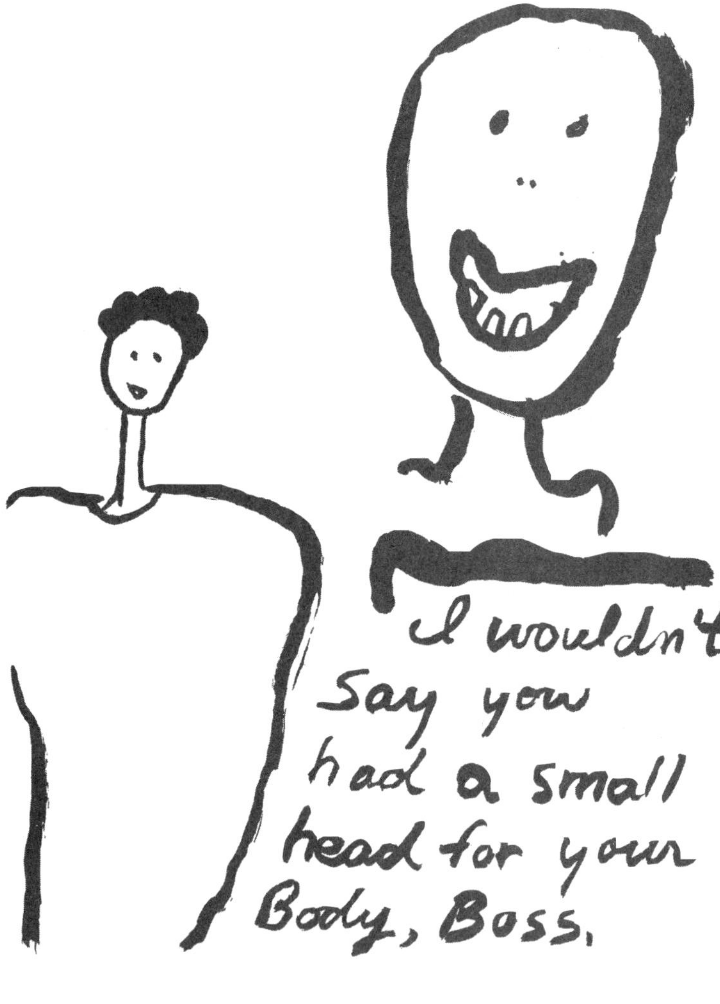

LIE

Telling the truth has the most disastrous consequences. What does telling the truth accomplish except peace of mind? What the hell does peace of mind do for you when you're trying to make a living? Really, what does telling the truth accomplish?

I say lie. Lie about your resume. Lie about where you have been. Lie about how good someone looks. Lie to take events to the extreme so that you are the good guy.

Lying is also the decent thing to do. Lie for yourself and the people you love. Movie stars, politicians, the media, our parents, all lie.

TIP:

If anyone ever questions you, just say, "Oh, I lied." Then laugh and say, "You believed me?"

*L*IVING IT UP seemed tame enough: a parody of the domestic do-it-yourself movement, something that certainly seemed ripe for parodying.

But as it happened, my publisher, Crown, was Martha Stewart's publisher as well. At first it didn't seem like this would be a problem. Just the opposite: it was suggested to me

LIVING IT UP 17

that she would be approached to write a blurb for the book jacket. But that was not to be. The book offended Martha Stewart, I was told. I was informed that, not only would Martha not be blurbing the book, but the book wouldn't be published by Crown at all. I started to laugh in disbelief when my editor broke the news. It was one thing to be worried about offending Jesse Helms or George Bush, but MARTHA!

When I asked what particularly in the book was offensive, I was told that Martha's people did not want her to be associated with feminine hygiene products. They were referring, specifically, to my instructions for making pine-needle-sachet underwear. All I could think of was, did they actually discuss all this at a meeting? I couldn't stop picturing the editorial staff of the house that had published *Ulysses*, sitting around arguing over whether pine-scented-underwear jokes were too controversial.

Maybe I really was going too far, but I called the writer's organization, PEN, which often provides legal help and advocacy for writers. I told them I was being censored and that this was a horrible precedent for the publishing world, that a publisher wouldn't print a dissenting view — of Martha Stewart! The PEN people listened politely to my story, and responded, "We usually handle authors who are about to be executed or who are imprisoned in a third world country." So I left Crown and went to Doubleday.

I still think publishing has changed, but then again, so has the ma and pa store, hand-packed ice cream, having your groceries delivered. All the things that Martha wants.

After Crown cancelled my book, it seemed like Martha was everywhere. Even in Grand Central Station on a gigantic banner, the only female between world leaders like Gorbachev, Clinton, and Bill Gates. One evening I saw Martha on the *Charlie Rose Show*. She said, "Charlie, what is wrong with American society is that we don't know how to grow a decent-tasting tomato or stack wood." If only Martha were right.

PINE NEEDLES

SO THE HOLIDAYS are over and you don't know what to do with those thousands of dried, prickly pine needles that are all over your house after Christmas? You find them under the radiator, under the chair, in the carpet. I've spent many hours from January until April pondering those beasties. I once spent an entire New Year's Eve thinking about what to do with those green devils, and the answer was—Underwear Sachets!

Sure they're un-comfortable, but they sure smell good. I like wearing them right when I get out of the shower. It gives you that extra freshness that you need.

Making them is easy. Take 2 pairs of underwear (try to make sure that they are the same size and *never* try to match a bikini with a brief), put one pair inside of the other and sew or staple the legs together, then stuff with the pine needles that you have swept up and then sew or staple together the waistbands.

I love to wear them and they're a good insurance policy if you've just eaten a plate full of beans and have too much gas. They act like an OdorEater for your pants.

Of course there are other projects to fill your time involving pine needles. I always get complaints from friends and neighbors telling me that they can't ever get all the pine needles up from the carpet. They say, "Karen, I've tried Christmas tree bags, power diesel vacuums, and hand-picking each needle.

I've made 2 pairs of Underwear Sachets for every person in my Rolodex, but it's July and I'm still picking up those damn needles!" Well, of course I've never had this problem, because I say—just leave the damn needles there! In fact, what I do is actually take in old pine trees from the curb, where others have thrown them out, and I shake all their old needles all over my house.

Accentuate! I put pine needles on the floor and in the corners. Sometimes I try to create hills and valleys of needles ranging from several inches to several feet. I have gotten very good at making pine-needle landscapes behind my furniture or right in the middle of the living room rug.

Have fun. Be creative. Soon you'll be hearing "I feel like I'm in the woods" from friends who visit your loft in the city even though you live in an industrial park. Then you'll know that you've made a very, very country home.

DO YOUR OWN CASKET

IT HAS BEEN during this bleak, dark month that got me thinking about the ulti-mate hibernation. I've come to realize that I just can't trust anyone to correctly organize my funeral after I'm gone. Many people fear death, but my biggest fear is that my last appearnce will be lying in an ordinary, nondescript, unmemorable casket. I want people walking away from my funeral with tears in their eyes, say-ing, "That was the most beautiful, amazingly decorated casket I've every seen."

The only way to ensure a funeral to my liking is to plan and rehearse my own funeral. People rehearse for weddings, take birthing classes, where they practice breathing, practice baking a cake till they get it just right. So every year I rehearse my funeral with me center stage. I send out invitations, and it has become an annual event with guests even sending funeral wreaths and flowers. I always update the ceremony to keep up with the latest funeral trends, although I'm having a great influence, I have to say, on funeral decora-tion. Let's get funerals and caskets a little more wild, please! A funeral direc-tor is going to tell me what the best-looking casket is? No way.

I design and do all the flowers for the rehearsal and invite my friends and family. It's a little hard on Mother, but I like the tears for effect. I also cook all the food and decide on the music—I want everything to be just right! And right means *my* way.

In my home I have a freezer just for food I make for my funeral party. You never can tell when the day will arrive, so it is good to be prepared. I always have a cake for 250 people just waiting in the wings of my freezer for that unexpected wedding or funeral. Then on the wedding cake, I decorate with fresh roses. I ice my funeral cake in a midnight-blue or dark purple and cover with dried roses. I love to go gothic for funerals! Select a theme for your big day. Try a come-as-you-are funeral, where guests come dressed as they are when they hear the news of your passing. Or do a medieval pageant or go Egyptian. Have your body wrapped as a mummy and design a menu with writ-ten instructions on the freezer bags. On the inside of the freezer lid I draw how

MAKING YOUR VERY OWN CASKET

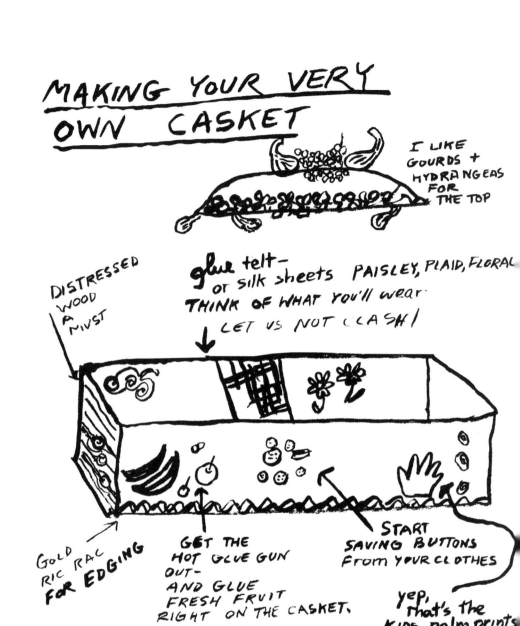

I LIKE GOURDS + HYDRANGEAS FOR THE TOP

DISTRESSED WOOD A MUST

glue felt- or silk sheets PAISLEY, PLAID, FLORAL THINK OF WHAT YOU'LL wear LET US NOT CLASH!

GET THE HOT GLUE GUN OUT - AND GLUE FRESH FRUIT RIGHT ON THE CASKET.

GOLD RIC RAC FOR EDGING

START SAVING BUTTONS FROM YOUR CLOTHES

yep, that's the KIDS palm prints + thumbprints

REMEMBER - TRY TO WEAR RED WHEN DEAD THE COLOR LOOKS GOOD ON A PALE BODY

I want the tables to look and write down what dishes to use with a marker.

I even make my own casket, and I'll share the plans with you right now. To make your own personal casket, lie on a piece of 4 x 8 plywood (make sure that it's a thick piece so that your dead weight doesn't make you fall through when they pick you up in it) and have a friend draw an outline of your body. Cut out a casket-type shape around the body outline, nail on some side pieces, and hinge another casket shape for the top, and you have a great base on which to decorate your own personalized casket. Now, why does a casket have to be a rectangle? Get creative. It's now or never. Try an outline of a body shape, a butterfly, an oval, a scalloped edge.

I've lined the inside of my casket with handmade velvet from France that I've bleached, dyed, and detailed with lace made by nuns in Belgium. I stained the exterior with a turquoise stain that I made up myself from my blue delphiniums. Next I spray-paint dried pasta and macaroni gold. I choose bows, wagon wheels, and elbows. Using my hot-glue gun reserved only for this occasion, I glue the macaroni in an abstract pattern. But you can arrange the macaroni to form words or sayings. And for that extra special, personal touch I dried some of the hydrangea from my garden and made an arrangement that will cover the top. It's more exquisite than any store-bought casket. I know the guests at my open-casket wake will appreciate the time and hard work that has gone into creating my final resting spot.

Next year I think I'm going to make my casket out of some old weathered-looking barn siding. I love the look of distressed wood, and I can't wait to hear everyone ask, "Where did you find that beautiful antique casket?" And I'll answer from my lying-down position, "I made it myself."

I tell myself I am visited by raspberries, strawberries, roses with names of Grandeur, Royalty and Impatience. Red lipstick kisses of flame, of crimson, of dawn and sunset. Sunsets from Norway midnight sun, northern forests with sun peaking from trees of pine.

I am luscious fabrics of calico from skirts + plaids of Scottish pipers.

I am a field of wildflowers. Lilacs, violets tulips of imperial elegance. Heather, lavender, irises. I am a bouquet for mankind.

I am visited by visions of heart, bleeding, warm and heartfelt. Purple + stain of courage and martyrdom.

I am a speckled wild cat with a coat of rare beauty.

POSITIVE ATTITUDE

MY LITERARY AGENT, Dino Mauritis, was sick. He had AIDS. He and his partner were close friends with Michael and me. Even though he was dying, Dino could find the joy in everyday living. He loved food, beautiful things, travel, and enjoying life.

INSTALLATIONS

18

He suffered from KS, Kaposi's sarcoma—a skin cancer that erupts in purple-red blotches all over the body. And the lesions on his body must have been so painful for someone with his sense of beauty. But what struck me was his civilized way of being. He always remained positive and looked forward to the next meal, a ride uptown, a new brand of cheese, a fresh bouquet of flowers.

In 1992 I was asked to play the role of Tom Hanks's doctor in the movie *Philadelphia*. In the film, Tom Hanks plays a gay attorney who has AIDS. Hanks's character is suffering from KS, too.

Ron Vawter, a member of the Wooster Group, was also in the film. He was suffering from the illness but still continued to work. Before Ron died we were doing readings of *Who's Afraid Of Virginia Woolf?* We wanted to get it produced and have Peter Sellers direct it. Even while we were talking about doing the project we knew it would never happen, but just doing the readings—living as if a future project would happen, and taking joy from the present moment—was the important thing.

So I became inspired with the idea for the installation *Positive Attitude*. I first made a preliminary drawing with a poem and images where the red and purple lesions were transformed into flowers, sunsets, and hearts.

In 1993, *Creative Time* asked me to make an installation on 42nd Street as part of the 42nd Street renewal project. I did the installation in an abandoned Papaya World right at 42nd St. and Broadway—one of the most populated intersections in the country, where 150,000 people from all parts of the world walk by every day.

I transformed the storefront with a new marquee that read "Positive Attitude" in large, Pepto-pink letters. Inside, there was a painted mural of a man, woman, and child, all suffering from KS. In the background was the poem, "Positive Attitude," some of which was translated into Spanish. Later, the poem went into my performance *American Chestnut*.

WHEN I WAS in eighth grade, I used to go to the Chicago Art Institute on Saturday mornings to take my weekly life-drawing class. After class, I'd wander the halls of the Institute, viewing the masters: Picasso, Van Gogh, Gauguin . . . almost all men. I longed for female mentors, and thought I had found them in Jean Dubuffet and Joan Miro who I believed were female. By the time I found out they weren't, it didn't matter to me; they had already served my purposes.

Years later, when I was at the San Francisco Art Institute, I found out there was to be a show by Judy Chicago at the San Francisco Museum of Modern Art. The exhibition would feature Chicago's piece *The Dinner Party*, a major work of feminist art. *The Dinner Party* is a huge triangular banquet table with place settings for famous women from all historical eras. Each setting is unique and fitting to the guest, interpreting the woman's accomplishments via a vaginal representation. Hundreds of women worked on the show, using traditional women's skills to make the tapestries, tablecloths, napkins, and all the other accoutrements.

You might think that, being a budding feminist artist with no female mentors or teachers, I would eagerly embrace *The Dinner Party*. But I didn't. I reacted against it. The problem, I felt, was that there would never be a show for famous men with their dicks interpreted as plates. You wouldn't see George Washington's dick interpreted as a cut-down cherry tree with the words "I always told the truth" embroidered on a napkin next to it. The whole piece was puzzling to me, and I created a reaction event, *The Prick Plates*, with my friend and performance collaborator Bruce Pollack. We hosted the event in front of the museum. The participants gathered in front of the museum with plates with the penises of famous men sculpted on them, and we staged an "opening" with wine and schmoozing.

In the early '90s, I was invited to create an exhibition at the San Francisco Art Institute—my alma mater. It seemed appropriate for

the piece to focus on my art education, and I decided to do a piece about the experience of being a female artist within the tradition of art education. While at the San Franciso Art Institute, I had worked at the library on Monday nights. In the library they had the most beautiful old wooden table—it was twelve feet long and four feet wide. I decided to use the table in the exhibition, along with books from the school's library.

I went through the library and selected art-related books and magazines. Some of them featured representations of women which exemplified the idea of the "male gaze." Others were by or about male artists whose life stories had some underlying, or overlying, misogynist component. I arranged the books and magazines on the table, and then placed plate glass over them. Then, with a red grease marker, I wrote my comments. Over a book on Gauguin, on one of his paintings of Tahitian women, I wrote, "The native woman is so inspiring. I left my wife and children to be inspired by the island!" On the famous Man Ray photo of a woman whose back is made to look like a cello, I wrote "HOW SURREAL!" And so on.

I wanted to show the dilemma of the female artist—the dilemma of appreciating art history and the contributions the artists like Gauguin and Man Ray, yet at the same time knowing that we, women, are the ones depicted, judged—that the work of art is created, in a sense, at our expense. This was my dilemma, and it is the dilemma of any woman in the art world or any female entering a museum or an art school. When I was a student there were no women at all in the the major textbook used for introductory art history courses: *The History Of Art.*

In the Spring of 1997 I was part of a show called *Sexual Politics* at UCLA's Armand Hammer Museum. The show's main purpose was to highlight and comment on *The Dinner Party.* "Moral History" had

been selected to be shown in the exhibition. As I was installing my piece at the museum, I met Judy Chicago. She was aware of the *Prick Plates* show I had done almost twenty years earlier. She told me that she thought it was important that I did the event, for it showed that the work could spark a dialogue with younger women and then a discourse could take place. She was very positive and inspiring to me.

THE RELAXATION ROOM

TODAY, MOTHERS-TO-be are expected to attain the "perfect birth." The expectant mother is made to feel that she is responsible for this, her baby's first experience of the world. The reality is that so much happens in the pregnancy and birth process that is beyond anyone's control—no matter how aware, responsible, and healthy a woman is. Nevertheless, if a woman has one glass of wine or one cup of coffee during pregnancy then she is made to feel that she is ruining her child's health. She must deny herself totally and give everything to the child. And if she has a C-section, she is made to feel that somehow she didn't do her best. I think this is a backlash, a punitive response to the fact that women increasingly have been putting off childbirth in favor of their careers.

And pregnant women today are given extensive instructions and coaching geared toward allowing them to give birth without expressing pain. There are relaxation exercises, Lamaze techniques, yoga, meditation. The idea of being serene and relaxed during childbirth is absurd to me. Labor was the most excruciating, painful experience my body has ever gone through. I had a natural childbirth and I broke my tailbone pushing my nine-pound daughter out of the birth canal. The idea that pain should not be expressed during childbirth is a cultural misogyny, a way of trying to control women's emotions.

After giving birth, I wanted to push the image of childbirth in my art. I realized that there aren't many images of childbirth in this culture. There are plenty of magazines where you can see a woman's pussy, of course, but you're not going to see a baby coming out of it. I wanted to do a piece that would expose the sexuality of childbirth, and that would confront viewers with the P-U-S-S-Y—that would say, "This is what it can do." I wanted something that would be visceral and vivid, like Frida Kahlo's childbirth paintings, but I wanted it to be a real picture, and I wanted it to be *big*.

My good friend Dr. Virginia Reath, a gynecologist, had found some photos of childbirth. She gave me three of them and I blew them up to 4 x 6 feet. They were graphic images of a baby's head crowning and emerging from the mother's vagina.

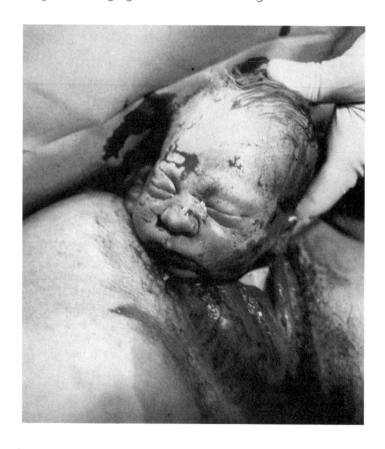

A DIFFERENT KIND OF INTIMACY

I hung the photos side by side in a room at the SFAI, near the "Moral History" installation. I stuck Post-Its with relaxation instructions ("Pretend you are floating on a cloud." "Picture yourself on the beach with your favorite beach towel." "Stay relaxed. This is for your baby.") all over the photos. I found these instructions so paternal, so patronizing, and under that, I felt that there was fear: fear of the female expressing her emotions.

This installation, "The Relaxation Room," also included a video of me squirting breast milk onto black velvet. I am in my studio, and I take my 40 D milk-laden breasts out of my smock and lactate on to the velvet in an abstract pattern. It's hysterical. It is my response to Jackson Pollack's film *I Am Nature*.

THE INTERNATIONAL SPIT BAR
AND THE SEXIST PIG CLUB

MICHAEL OVERN

The International Spit Bar at the Kitchen.

I WANTED TO do a piece about different countries and the way they interact, about xenophobia and prejudice. This "International Spit Bar," which I constructed at the Kitchen in 1992, displays small flags from countries around the world. Viewers are offered glasses of red wine and are invited to spit the wine onto the flag of their choice.

Along with the International Spit Bar, I also did a piece called the "Sexist Pig Club." In a corral, similar to what you'd find at a county fair, a male artist draws a nude or partially-clad woman. She is posed by the artist, and we watch him staring and drawing the female.

The Sexist Pig Club at the Kitchen.

MICHAEL OVERN

THE AMERICAN CHESTNUT was the most abundant tree in America until the early-twentieth-century, when a blight almost rendered the trees extinct. The blight prevents chestnut trees from maturing—they remain in a sort of perpetual puberty, sending up shoots, but never blooming. "In its struggle to live,

19

THE AMERICAN CHESTNUT

it dies," my landlady said as she showed us the chestnut on the property around our house in Nyack.

The chestnut paneling that encased the windows, doors, and moldings in the Nyack house resonated with something very deep in my being. I became interested in the trees on the property. I started sketching the American chestnut often.

The story of the demise of the American chestnut reminded me of the elm tree blight in Chicago when I was growing up. At that time, I had felt as if the dying, leafless trees that lined the boulevards were symbols of the soldiers dying in Vietnam.

I started to work on a project focusing on the parallels between illnesses of nature and illnesses of society. In 1993, I received a Guggenheim fellowship for the project. It was a much-needed boost, financially and morally.

SYLVI DE SWAAN

A DIFFERENT KIND OF INTIMACY

I wanted to create a work that would be installation-like but which would also resemble performance works of the seventies. Every segment of the project, *The American Chestnut*, has its own unique visuals, with my body fitting into a slide or video projection. This creates the affect of a series of tableaux vivants.

I knew that when *The American Chestnut* premiered, it would get a lot of media attention, because of all the publicity surrounding the ongoing court case. I wanted to premiere the work somewhere that could handle the situation. I had shown my work at the American Repertory Theatre at Harvard on several occasions, and I had been supported by manager Rob Orchard and artistic director Bob Brustein at critical times. When I asked if I could do the piece there, they said yes. They also let me use the libraries for much of my reseach and writing.

American Chestnut is more technically complicated than my prior performances. It incorporated several videos. One was the nursing/action-painting video. There was also a videotape of "Museum," a performance where I walked through a museum nude and posed in front of nude sculptures, imitating them. Like the nursing video, it was meant to be funny.

MICHAEL OVERN

Before the show premiered, someone from the NEA called the American Repertory Theatre, inquiring about my nursing video, asking for a detailed description of it. The NEA wanted to know if this new show was "indecent." The ART staff considered it odd. They had never had inquiries about other shows.

MICHAEL OVERN

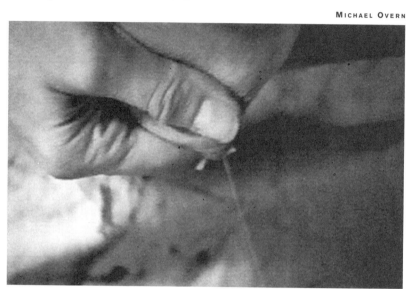

The day of the *American Chestnut* premier, I was told that there had been a letter with a threat to my life. Harvard was not taking the threat lightly, and I was told that I was to be given a police escort. There were going to be police in the wings during the performance, in the entrance to the theater, and in plain clothes in the audience. I was beside myself. I didn't know if I could go through with the show. I sat with my husband and talked it over. It's still difficult to look back and remember that this was the decision I was being forced to make on the opening night of the show—whether to risk my life or not.

I decided that I had to perform—if I didn't, it would be like letting them kill me in a different way.

Ben Brantley, the theater critic of the *New York Times*, was coming up to Cambridge to review the performance. There was some discussion about telling him not to come. I had been concerned from the beginning about it, because it seemed like such a far way to travel to review a show. My agent had felt that it would be better if Brantley waited for the show to play New York. And now, with the pressure of the death threat, I was even more nervous at the idea of Ben Brantley being in the audience. But I decided that, if I was going to be shot on stage, I might as well have the *New York Times* there. So Brantley came to the premiere. He later wrote that "no one projects pain with the visceral intensity of Ms. Finley." It was definitely true that evening.

When I left the stage at the close of the show, a policewoman, gun on hip, escorted me to my dressing room. A few minutes later, as I was undressing, Bob Brustein and Rob Orchard knocked on my door, saying, "Karen, are you decent?" I knew that they didn't mean what it sounded like they meant, but at that moment it was just too much. I answered, "No, I'm not," and sat down and cried.

As I left the theater that night, Michael and I heard sirens and, as we got closer to the little house where we were staying, we saw an ambulance and fire engine sitting outside. I was terrified and I ran up the stairs to my daughter. But it turned out that it had been a false alarm, and nothing to do with us.

Before I premiered *The American Chestnut*, I would get upset if things didn't go as planned on stage. I had always felt that, if a performance was going to work the way it should, I needed total support from my artistic director and from technicians. If I didn't have this support, I felt, my show was in danger of collapsing. But with *The American Chestnut*, I realized that this dream of total support was never going to come true, and that my show was going to collapse — that it was going to be in a constant state of collapse.

I was thinking of Frank Gehry's architecture, his buildings that embrace collapse — that are designed as if the earthquake has already happened. I became very inspired, and my performance style evolved. I started to focus on the idea of embracing collapse. I no longer felt that my shows had to be cleanly directed, in perfect working order. Instead, I wanted to present work that was anti-finished, anti-polished. I wanted to show the performance as a living process. I read from the script, left the stage to go to the toilet, changed costumes on stage—did everything I could to break down the myth of the fourth wall, of the "perfect moment." To focus on structure, on formal concerns, and not on politics was my struggle.

VACUUMING

TONIGHT, I WAS going to tell you how I stayed up til five A.M. because my daughter couldn't sleep. I used to stay up til dawn five nights a week, 'cause I was a hipster—a cooler—a tanker—a swanker—on the scene. Making the scene. "So," I said to myself, as I'm watching Piglet and Eeyore and Winnie the Pooh, "I'll just pretend I'm on the third floor of Danceteria and that I'm watching a cartoon in the S&M bar, the Hundred-Acre Wood."

Winnie the Pooh—now there's a case of an eating disorder if I ever saw one. That Hundred-Acre Wood sure has a psychological profile. Tigger manic depressive or hyperactive, Rabbit passive aggressive, Eeyore just plain depressed with self-esteem problems, Piglet insecure, with a speech impediment. Owl: delusions of grandeur. And Christopher Robin, the enabler.

Winnie The Pooh. Isn't that a girl's name for a boy bear? Don't you wonder about that pooh, poopoo, shit thing going on there? Hi, I'm pooh. Hi, I'm I'm a piece of shit. I can just imagine them all at the Dungeon, with Winnie in chaps. Piglet is in some corner being peed on by Tigger. Eeyore is having the tail pinned on his heiny, saying "Could you nail that tail in my butt a *little* slower . . . and harder . . . Christopher Robin?" Chris has some police gear on and he's using his riding crop.

I was watching Beatrix Potter and I swear to god I saw Tom Kitten's butthole. I want to see that purple dinosaur's butthole now!

I'm the kind of parent that goes all the way with Barney for my daughter. Barney sheets, blankets, pillowcases, placemats, purses, stroller. (I feel it is important to a child's development for the child to adore something the parent hates.) That's Barney the dinosaur, not Barney's the store. There's no such thing as a Barney's stroller.

I'd love to buy a Barney's onesie. But when I walked into Barney's, I immediately realized that they didn't have a children's section. When my daughter needed to nurse while I was trying something on, the saleswoman started yelling at me, "Don't do that here!"

I responded, "Nursing is fashionable."

She said, "Don't you dare change your baby here!"

And I said, "I think you have some unresolved sexual tension."

And she said, "Don't accuse me of being scatterbrained."

Then another salesperson came in and said, "Oh, ignore old Margaret Thatcher. She's the only man in the cabinet."

And I said, "That's a sexist thing to say."

And a customer said, "Can you blame her? Would you trust the chocolate-smeared woman changing her baby in your dressing room?"

So the pilot shot down in Bosnia has found God. He says, "God saved me." I don't think sucking your sock sweat to survive is God saving you.

I don't think eating cow-pee grass to survive is God saving you.

I don't think licking ant hills to survive is God saving you.

God always gets into it.

To me, God getting into the act is finding a six-pack of Diet Coke, some reefer and—Scotty, beam me up!

To me, god getting into the act is getting the war over with—

stopping the murder, the rape, the genocide, the ethnic cleansing.

God doesn't get involved there.

That's God for you.

God knows a media opportunity when he sees one.

The woman who lost two children in the Oklahoma City bombing just had her tubes untied so she could have more children. The doctor and the hospital are performing the surgery for free. When the woman heard the news she said "It was just a gift from God." Gee, wasn't that nice of God to finally show up.

You know, God is to blame for a lot of things.

Everyone blames TV, books, music, Hollywood, artists like me.

There are wars fought in the name of God.

Killings, murders in the name of God.

God told me to do it.

*   *   *

The Bible told me to do it.

If we are to censor anything, I think we should start with God.

I meet two young Bosnian Muslim men. They are attending school here. Their mother is a teacher and she started a business that employed women. Their mother is a Moslem and a feminist.

The mother owned a factory that employed women. She employed a young Serbian woman who wanted to go to school. Their mother lent the employee money and encouraged her to go to school.

During the war, their mother was captured and was to be killed. She was in the truck. She sat next to the driver who was to kill her. It turned out that he was the brother of the Serbian woman who she encouraged to go to school. The driver said he would not kill her, but would instead bring her to a concentration camp.

And her two young sons, boys really, felt this was a miracle.

Being in a concentration camp is no miracle.

This is God showing up?

I'm at the playground. There are two boys, aged four and six, and they start kicking another boy. The boy who is being kicked—his parents are there. And the two boys who are kicking, their mother is there.

The mother of the boy who was kicked says, "We are trying to teach our son not to fight with his body, but to use words." The mother of the two boys who kicked says, "I used to think that, but they are rough boys and other kids were fighting, so I just let them fend for themselves. It's important for boys to be able to fight."

The boys who had kicked were on the slide. A little baby girl had crawled onto the slide and was enjoying herself. The boys ran up the slide the wrong way and the baby was stuck. The baby's mother removed her daughter. One of the boys on the slide shouted, "I'll kiss your fucking ass. I'll kiss your fucking ass. I'll beat your fucking ass." His mother said, "They don't know what they are saying." I think they know exactly what they are saying.

IRIS'S

HELLO, MAY I have the reference desk? Yes, this being the eighteenth of May, I'm calling to inform you that the black walnut tree, the last tree to grow its leaves in spring, has finally done so.

Well, the head librarian is on vacation.

Well, make sure you write it down.

DONA ANN McADAMS

A DIFFERENT KIND OF INTIMACY

First let me introduce you to the time.

It was a time when everyone had gardens. It was a time when the social calendar was set by the first plant sale given by the village garden club. It was a time when the flowering, weeping cherry was at the height of pinkness. Let us stand beneath the flowering cherry and look upon the sky. It was an exceptional year for all flowering trees, because the winter before had been terrible. This was the time of the daffodil, but still too early for the lilac.

Let me tell you about the place.

The town had a library, a post office, and it had a shrine devoted to all plant life. On a prominent corner there was a cardtable with a blue tablecloth. Here, for two hours on Thursday and Saturday, questions would be answered on difficult problems of the garden. Woodchucks, the blight of the maple tree. Proper tree and shrub pruning.

Yes, they all had beautiful hands.

Hands that worked in soil, and planted seedlings, that collected pine needles for bedding, that made trellises so trumpet vines and morning glories and clematis would grow.

It was known in the growing community that the most beautiful hands belonged to Mr. Dove. Mr. Dove was 92, soon to be 93, and he was an iris grower. His hands were thick and calloused from 70-some years of handling, separating and attending the iris.

Now, mind you, iris growers and day-lily growers are a generous type. Probably because of the plants' abundance and ability to multiply. Not like a rose grower. The rose is a competitive flower of awards, ribbons, and honors.

When people went to Mr. Dove's iris farm to order bulbs for the next year, they would walk through the beds and beds of irises with a paper and pencil, making their selections.

Portrait of Larry

Vanity

Carolina Gold

Proud Tradition

Latin Lover

First Violet

World News

Dauntless

Ramses

The requests would be given in May, Memorial Day weekend, when the irises were at their peak. And the unearthed iris bulbs with their attached leaves would be picked up in August.

Mr. Dove would handwrite the names of the irises on the leaves. On the other side of the leaf would be written "M.O.S." for "My Only Son."

This was the only way Mr. Dove could endure Memorial Day, since his son was declared missing in action on May 31.

MICHAEL OVERN

THOMAS

My lover died 6 weeks ago
but I haven't cried yet.
I'm a man who was taught to keep a stiff upper lip.
All day long I drink my tea.
All day long, cup of of tea, a cupper.
I still make a cup for him.
I make it just the way he likes it—2 sugars and lots of cream. In his special cup
with Puck and Midsummer Night's Dream.

Every day I open his cologne and splash it in the air.
Every day I read the Living section and put it on his chair.
Every night I open the window. Even though I always get cold,
he liked it so.
I fluff up the eiderdown we bought for our second anniversary.
I haven't had time yet to change the sheets.
I run the bath and light candles and pretend we are together for the very first
time.
Something restrained.
Dark oak and half-slices of magnolia on ice.
I think the gin is settling in.

It's been 7 weeks since you've been gone,
But there is something, sweetheart, I must tell you.
Your rocking chair is going to have to go.
It just must leave the room,
Tomorrow I begin to redecorate with new colors.
I do hope you trust me.
You always do.
So when I come home from holiday I can start anew.

There is so much to do.

The hangers, your shirts, your letters, your mail, our life.

Maybe I'll keep the rocking chair just a little bit longer.

It's been 8 weeks and 2 days since you left me, and I'm certainly trying to keep busy.

You know all the beautiful things I can do with my hands.

I make curtains so lovely that when you look out your window it is even lovelier.

I make a chair more comfortable—a joiner, a plumber, a jack of all trades.

Now that I've reminded you of my talents—

of what I can do with my hands—

Now that I've shown you how delightful I am with strangers—

Now that I've demonstrated how well I am in conversation—

I think I'll have a cup of tea and get on with it.

But the pain is in going on.

The pain is in surviving.

I said to myself, again, Oh, Thomas—have a cup of tea and get on with it.

But tonight I couldn't.

I turned on the music loud and danced and danced and danced.

I went and saw all the friends I could.

And when I got home—

The rocking chair is still his.

A vacant chair.

A vacant place at the table.

A vacant space in the bed.

And in the back of the wardrobe,

I missed a shirt, his shirt

hidden under mine,

and in the pocket was a note.

Leave everything to Thomas.

You've left me everything.

You've left me everything.

Worn at the edge—

his thumbprint, his writing,

and I sat in the rocking chair and I just lost it.

I just lost it.

I just lost it.

A DIFFERENT KIND OF INTIMACY

WORMS

THE FATHER'S LYING in his bed, watching TV, lying in his underwear. It's Saturday night. His 2 little girls are asleep in their rooms. The 16-year-old daughter is reading in her room.

The house is surrounded by squad cars. They break down the door, handcuff the father, put a gun to his head, put a gun to the 16-year-old's head. "You move and I'll blow your brains out." The little girls pee on themselves, they are so scared. "We're going to get you, nigger! Where's the drugs, bitch? Your daddy's a scum, a cross dressing, stealing, lying, murdering animal. Honey, you are a crack smoking whore. Where's the drugs? In your asshole? In your cunt? Is it in your girls' assholes? We're going to take it out. We're just going to have to smash up the furniture, the mattresses, the toys."

The family sees its possessions torn apart.

Then a policeman whispers in the sergeant's ear, "Wrong address."

FACE LIFT

MAY I HAVE the reference desk. Hello, I wanted to bring this to your attention. There was only one sockeye salmon spotted in the Columbia River this year.

Yes, well, I was just reading about Anne Boleyn writing her name on the walls of the Tower of London. I'll make a note of it. I am having lunch with my friend so I must run along now. Goodbye.

Beatrice decided something had to be done about Lily's face. The skin under her chin was sagging. Finally Beatrice said to her, "Why don't you try a lift? The competition out there just must be awful."

"Well, yes, the competition is awful. I was thinking of going back to school or trying out for the Pillsbury Bakeoff with my plum torte. Or maybe I should just join a convent."

"This isn't a joke, Lily. You don't think your ex-husband took off with that girl because of her *accomplishments*, do you? Look, I'm your very best friend and I have to tell you—when I look at your face—you're ugly. You're old. A new face is a new start. A new face is a new you. When you get your eyes done, put a little collagen in those lips, you'll at least be able to have someone look at you and not think about their mother."

In the tortoiseshell hand mirror that had been her grandmother's, Lily looked at her image. Her eyes, the laugh lines from her children's pranks, the creases from untimely deaths and from surviving.

I can't erase my memories.

I can't erase my life.

LINGERIE

WHEN NICKY WALKED out of the library to go to lunch, she knew it would be difficult to be taken seriously, to be left alone.

"Baby, I like those titties. Baby, I like your ass. Come on over here Mama. Kiss kiss kiss kiss."

"Come here pussy puss puss puss."

"Excuse me—What am I—some animal? Some cat you're calling? Who the hell are you talking to? When I walk down the street, do you have to comment about my body?"

"Lady—bitch, I'm flattering you!"

"Saying 'Come here pussy puss puss' and wagging your tongue is not flattery."

"You fucking bitch! You ugly cocksucking whore!"

This was the reason Nicky was so concerned about her image. She didn't want to be looked at as Pussy Galore—one of James Bond's girls. She wondered where they were now, those actresses.

Nicky was in the diner deep in thought, when she said aloud, "Why couldn't James Bond show his bulge, his ass-crack cleavage?"

Everyone in the diner looked at her and Nicky spilled her orange juice all over her chest. A male detective rushed over and began wiping her chest with a napkin. "Let me help clean you up. This is my area of expertise. HA HA HA HA HA HA HA."

Nicky kept this moment in mind. Humor and humiliation are very similiar.

Later that night she dreamt of James Bond wearing pants that exposed his ass cheeks, wrapping his privates, pushing up his genitalia, squeezing together his testicles, form-fitting his wrapped penis in lace, balls exposed in tight fitting contraptions with snaps and cup sizes.

Men's clothes need to be eroticized.

I want to see men's nipples. I want to see men photographed so we can see the tips of their nipples, hard and erect, on the cover of *Time*. I want little see-through panels across their chests.

I want clothing that draws attention to a man's scrotum. I want testicles dressed in nice, wooly caps. I want the hot, hairy ball look. I want high-heeled oxfords and Nikes so the butt goes up in the air, so I can grab booty. I want to smell booty.

I want to see the penis in a constant state of erection—and I want that interpreted by fashion NOW. And if that means banana or salami appliques sewn on the crotch, or the wiener actually taken out of the confines of the trouser and dressed in haute couture, I'm ready for it!

In the same way that women's suits have shoulder pads, giving the feeling of big-shouldered male power, men should wear falsies sewn into their work shirts to give the illusion of nurturing, adaptability, and the right to be humiliated.

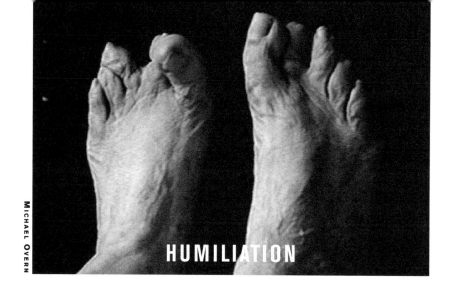

HUMILIATION

MICHAEL OVERN

TONITE, I DON'T tell you of the stabbing, the knife wound. Tonite, I don't tell you of the punch of the fist. Tonite, I speak of the pain of laughter, the butt of jokes, the Human Punchline.

I'm the child who vomited and the teacher had me wipe up my own puke with my shirt—and you're all laughing.

I'm that girl who wet her panties and was made to sit in her urine all day.

Give me a special hiding place so I can hide my shame and disgrace.

I remember the laughter—children being called dummy and stupid, not having money for school clothes, body fat, faces pimply, bangs cut too short, hair sticking up or out, farts, the thick mucous of sleepiness, the child in me not knowing what is appropriate, when to laugh.

Let me tell you of life's finer moments.

Finer Moment is 12 years old. And she's our mascot. The boys would snap Finer's bra from behind, like a rubberband. We're all laughing at her child-big breasts. Call them hooters, honkers, bazoombas, boobies. Titty mamma, cow woman, mama mammary glands. Oh, the artwork that was created in her honor—at her development's expense. Bosoms cartooned so long they dragged on the floor and wrapped around her neck like a noose, to die for. Cleavage so deep you could drown. That female body was beginning to be dangerous. Give me a special hiding place so I can hide my shame and disgrace.

Ain't had enough?

Ain't had enough yet?

You want the physical evidence, alright—

Physical Evidence was only in diapers and she wouldn't stop crying—and so I beat Physical—and beat and beat Physical and she wouldn't stop. I call Jesus, I call the president—he was beaten as a child—he died on the cross. I call the pastor, the priest.

Beat the devil out of Physical.

So I beat Physical all day but she never stops crying. Later, I realize that it was the sound of my fist crushing her ribs—so I must have gotten the devil out. Must have got the devil out.

Let me tell you about the lesson.

When he vomited, the only way I could teach him was for him to clean up his own puke himself.

Yes, he was puking while he was cleaning it up.

I left the room awhile because what I want is the name calling, the humiliation.

That's the way I control my classroom.

I don't want to look backward.

I don't want to look forward.

Just keep me where I am.

Keep the birthday candles burning.

Push the face into the icing.

Tie her up in her ribbon.

Force feed him.

Starve her.

Rock me, rock me, rock me.

Whose child was a thing, a thing, a thing,

a petting object,

a catalogue number,

an outfit,

a gift—a reason to buy things.

The mother sat her down. "You can't play sports. There is no team for you." She ran. She jumped. She climbed. "You'll never be as good as a boy. Your hair will get in the way."

She went to her room and took her mother's shears and cut her hair off. Her mother sat her down.

"I did that too when I was your age. I cut off my hair just like you. But you can't fight being a woman."

"But mother I'm not fighting. I'm just being me."

"Don't argue with me. In order to attract men, you should never appear stronger than boys."

All she has to look forward to is a hairdo.
A nail salon.
So I scratch you with my beauty—
My beauty is my weapon.
She couldn't be smart—
She'd be sassy.
She couldn't have opinions—
She'd be called angry.
She couldn't have power—
She'd become nagging.

When Nicky got to school everyone laughed. Her mom had tried to give her self-inflicted haircut a name. "Tell them it is a pixie, a bob. Tell them you are trying to look like Twiggy."

But her hair looked like freshly mowed grass with the tracks of the lawn mower in it.

Nicky liked running her hand through her hair because it felt like a magic carpet.

"My head is a magic carpet," she told the teacher.

The teacher called Nicky's mother.

"Nicky is lying. She says her hair is a magic carpet."

"We'll take care of it, Miss Davis."

Later that night, when her father came home, her parents took turns beating her with her mother's hairbrush because she had lied.

Give me a special hiding place so I can hide my shame and disgrace.

David is holding the turtle he saved and saved for. A 49-cent turtle that he bought at the shopping center. David carries his new pet under his shirt. He's not worried about himself. He's thinking about his turtle. Keeping his turtle warm. Those three children were cold but the boy wasn't going to let another creature feel like he felt.

Let me tell you of life's finer moments—

Give me a secret hiding place where I can hide my shame and disgrace.

Hello. Yes, reference desk. I have something vital to your records. The cow bird never sees her eggs hatch, never hears their cries for food. Since the cow bird lives off of the bugs that live on the roaming cattle, she is never in one place long enough to nest. Therefore, she lays her eggs in other birds' nests. This is the only way her young can survive.

DAVID

Here is the journey we all must go through,
though none of us will live to tell.
Here lies the journey we all must take,
though all of us find our own way.
Even though we whisper—Let go,
even though we lead the hand over the fence—
One's own spirit, soul, must leave when it is ready—
to the light
and through the tunnel.

While you were on your deathbed

you fretted about who would take care of your loved ones when you were gone.

Even in that moment you thought more about others than yourself.

Requests, Resolutions, Absolutions, Confession.

These are all words of forgiveness, of I'm sorry.

These are things people ask of themselves at death—but you asked them of us and yourself your entire life.

You did not need this illness to transgress, transcend, transform,

for you required that in all of your relationships and creativity.

Life for you was a profound, intimate quest to change your pain into compassion.

We knew why he wouldn't die—

because we knew he wouldn't trust the beauty of the other side. He would want to stand, smoke a cigarette and ponder and think awhile.

To make creations of words and art and beauty.

A church was created in his honor,

with flowers and music.

Prayer provided.

None answered.

African violets, peonies, bachelor buttons, angel hair, and lemon rice—

petunias, new sheets with sweet smells of hay and wheat grass.

Lemon verbena too.

Make the kisses strong, I won't be here long.

Make the mouth settle, for I'll be going soon.

Make the breath slow for I don't have many left.

Make the day beautiful for it may be my last.

Some people need help in their journey.

It is a journey that doesn't require steps.

No, not by air, ship, or rail.

No, not by phone or wire.

Here lie the memories of one who had a good life.
He loved and he was loved back.
He didn't die alone. Still he died too young.
Tell me—We will all be dead one day.

He said,
I don't think I'm the star of this movie.

Answered back,
But you have been the star of other movies.

He asked,
Do I die at the end of the movie?

Answered back,
I haven't seen the ending yet.

He asked,
How will I die?

Why don't you try it in your sleep.

The love so strong. The emotions so loaded. The mysteries still behold us.
Beyond a life—Beyond this—

Time and emotions stood still in their intensity,
like a floodgate, like a too-full balloon.
I'm disappearing, I'm disappearing, I'm disappearing, he said.
You will become something else, Tom said.
David always said death is just the dispersal of energy.

A CAKE

I AM SO RELIEVED. The party will be a success now that I know the cake to make. Now, the only problem with summer birthdays are conflicting vacations. And I certainly hope it is not too hot.

Lily wiped an imagined sweat droplet from her brow. Thinking about the cake was so pleasurable. She could see it in her mind's eye. Perfectly shaped, creamy and cool, with lovely elegant slices. The cake would have pale pink and orange roses with moss-green leaves and stems with graceful script handwriting: HAPPY BIRTHDAY BEATRICE. It would be placed on a silver doily.

Lily stared through her kitchen window at the apple tree that her now-dead father had saved by pouring cement into its roots. Beside the apple tree was an American chestnut tree, a poor tree that looked like a struggling youngster even though it was nearly 100 years old.

I'll never leave my trees. They've seen everyone I've loved and everyone I haven't loved.

Lily liked to bake cakes. She baked cakes for the children she lost. For the birthdays they would have celebrated. Their graduations, communions.

Wesley, 7 years old, rheumatic fever. Sarah, stillborn. Molly, scarlet fever and whooping cough. Stella, her mother, T.B.; her brother Ed, polio; and Constantine, her grandson, AIDS.

POSITIVE ATTITUDE

Gentle gentle man
wearer bowlers
and old things
things of eras past
you preferred—
You made us remember the things in life
That made living so special.

Dinners of tenderloin and cranberry rind
Deserts of chiffon soufflés and chocolate cremes
Holidays of haunted houses, perfumed candles and tea rooms.
Exotic, expensive
my body smelled of jasmine when around you

Tell me about Greece
The ancient and the wise
Tell me about France
the lace the linen the grape
Tell me about England the tweeds the teas the customs
The man with the bowler hat
Every occasion made festive
by your appearance
Every conversation made civil by your point of view
Gentle gentle man
how do I live without you?

I visit the festival of lights
        and remember how they would light up your eyes
Yes, the tree is so lovely

I slurp from soup spoons
with handles of rare metals pounded
into lion manes and serpents' tongues
Yes, the chowder is lovely
    I plan a trip to a forgotten castle
A place I'll never go
but the dreams make the ugly days pass quicker
    I buy gifts that take me so long to buy—
the rose has to be so perfect
the cheeses aged just right
Oh, the shopping was so exhausting
but so wonderful
I can't take your positive attitude. I can't take your looking on the bright side. When your body is covered with speckled spots of disease. You just turn your marked torso over to me and whisper in my ear—these words.

I tell myself that I am visited by raspberries, strawberries, with names of Grandeur, Royalty, and Impatience. Red lipstick kisses of flame, of crimson of dawn and sunset.

I am luscious fabrics of calico from skirts and plaids of Scottish pipers.

I am visited by visions of hearts, bleeding, warm, and heartfelt. Purple and stoic and martyrdom.

I am a field of wildflowers. Lilacs, violets, tulips of imperial elegance. Heather, lavender, irises.

I am a bouquet for all mankind.

I am a speckled wild cat with a coat of rare beauty.

I dreamed we were in a small room. Between us was a stack of construction paper. With my paper I made lists of ways to get out of the room. When my head came out of my to-do list there was Constantine, sitting at the table that he had made from the papers. From foiled gum wrappers he made silver candle sticks, from a brown bag, a mahogany table, both in the style of empire. He cut out the finest porcelain china from shirtboards. Then he snapped his hands off at his wrists to make us our own wine goblet.

Crystal, of course.

Since his hands were gone he asked me to unzip his chest,

and from his heart flowed a red-velvet burgundy.

I brought the glass to his lips and he took a swallow. I had wine like this the day I met Julia Child.

Remember, he said, it isn't that you lived but how you lived.

Then he said, I think I'll think about dessert.

Then he was gone.

We will all be getting out of here one day.

But while we are waiting,

let us have something sweet.

CHANDLER'S

HELLO, REFERENCE DESK. I thought you'd be interested in this information about sheep. The reason sheep have their tails docked is that, when their tails are long, they get into their feces and attract flies. The flies lay eggs, which turn into maggots, which burrow into the sheeps' skins. The maggots particularly like the moist areas of the sheep, such as the rectum and eyes. That is most painful.

I'm sorry, but because of a budget deficit our reference desk will no longer be available. This is a recording.

Lily was stunned. She took a walk to her second-favorite spot, Chandler's Stationery and Books and Office Supplies.

There was no place as romantic for her as a stationery store. She would go through the endless aisles of pastel Post-Its, lined notecards, and patterned notebooks, poetic greeting cards, foiled giftwraps. The smells of the papers intoxicated her into a levitated state of absolute bliss.

But it was not until later, when her husband left her for a college girl some fifteen or twenty years his junior, that she began taking her visits to Chandler's more seriously. At first it was just looking—feeling very gently the onion-skinned papers of pink and blue. Or her favorite pen, a Lindy broadpoint that came in black and brown and purple.

Once, as she was looking at a display of bookmarks, she felt her skin shiver. It was just too exciting, feeling the leather between her fingers—she climaxed right there on the spot. And with every bookmark she touched she climaxed again and again. She came in daily now.

Once, she saw her ex-husband, and his new wife, with child, looking at birth announcements. Even though Lily was only three feet away, they took no notice of her.

She went to the woman's room and wrote in a Chandler's composition notebook specifically created for the University student:

A DIFFERENT KIND OF INTIMACY

"I know you like your cunts young. You are in a constant search for your own immortality, a potential mother for your namesake. You cover up your fear of breastfeeding by pinching my nipples hard so they bleed instead of lactate.

"I could never tell you my fear of having a malformed baby with gills or webbed feet and a tail.

"Being pregnant means accepting the fear of the unknown.

"I'm vagina dentata, a cunt with molars and biters and cutters."

"I think you dropped this," she said, as she handed her poem to her ex-husband.

She wanted to make love, not in a bedroom or in a car or on a beach or a sofa, but in a literary setting where the writer's tools congregate. In a stationery store. She wanted to perform erotic acts surrounded by old books, in a public library, among shelves and magazines and people who used literature as a pastime—who wrote letters and had diaries.

BACKS

"THAT WAS THE best show I ever saw" said Nicky, turning off the TV. "What a great idea, to have a cop show with Emma Peel, Charlie's Angels, Angie Dickinson, Cagney and Lacey—and instead of pulling out guns, they open their legs to show their vaginas dentata—and then just snap the criminal. That's something even T.J. Hooker can't do."

Tonight, I'm trying to have a good time. Tonight, I'm trying to have a good time.
Tonight, I'm going to keep my eyes open—
Because when I close them—our sisters' blood calls us.
It is all too painful.
The water is deeper.
Now we are drowning.
The tears of hopelessness—it won't go away—
the hot baths taken to soothe the broken limbs,
the showers hot and stinging to wash their hands away.
The trickle of water
becomes a stream,
the stream becomes a chain of lakes,
the lakes become oceans
from blood emptied out.
The Red Sea.
That's why we call the sea *la mer.*
That's why we call the earth mother earth.
That's why all ships are she.
Understanders of tears,
of battles never won but fought again and again.

I hate all sports.
Once I loved a game.

But the only game a woman is allowed is to be hunted,

to be chased.

I'm so glad I'm getting older—so I'm not so pretty anymore.

So I'm not so pretty anymore.

Last night I stood on the corner of Wooster St. I saw 3 men on the street. I waited and waited before entering my car. I locked the car and drove fast. I looked in the back seat. But that is nothing special for me. Nothing special for me.

Then there are the elevators, the stairways, or just being home.

That is the sport a woman can play.

The lookout, the chase, the hunt, the tackle, the grab.

I'm nothing but a goal, a score, a touchdown, a homerun.

You see, she was his trophy.

And I'm waiting for the football star to publicly mourn,

to publicly grieve for his wife, the mother of his 2 children.

Next time hit her harder. Next time hit her harder, harder.

Next time hit her harder.

I never wanted to be a cheerleader.

I'm a nice person; I'd cheer for the other team.

A girl can't grow up to be a team player.

NO MATTER HOW GOOD SHE IS SHE IS NEVER GOOD ENOUGH.

That is why girls get pregnant—

because it's one thing boys can't do.

For a first lady, finding the right problem is a must. Hillary finally found the right problem. Her husband.

She wasn't as fat or old as Mrs. Bush and they keep telling us that is our problem.

She wasn't as skinny, bitchy, mean to her kids, or obsessed with designer clothes as Nancy Reagan. She wasn't a drug addict alcoholic with breast cancer like Betty Ford.

They wanted to see her break down, publicly. They wanted to see her cry and say, "I can't take it—I can't take it—I can't take it." They wanted her to say,

"I'm sorry that I'm smarter than Bill. I'm sorry I was first in my class at Yale Law School and Bill was sixth. I was a fool to change my name but you know what fools women are!"

They wanted her to start redecorating the White House like Jackie. They wanted her to have a litterbug program, a wildflower program. They wanted her to be the first lady of cleaning and gardening, like Lady Bird.

They wanted her neck to become so strained it looked like constant whiplash, always on the verge of tears, holding it in, like Pat Nixon.

They wanted her to be humble, and sweet, with a whispery voice and small steps, so good, like Rosalyn.

That is why we have Martha Stewart. She has the perfect haircut and she makes all of her important decisions in domestic territory.

This unattainable domestic ideal is the underbelly of the only appreciation a woman really gets, from her clean house, her shopping lists, her overpampered nails, her put-together meals.

She needs to be sweeping, washing, cleaning, polishing, dusting, buffing, drying, waxing.

She has to be stirring, mixing, beating, whipping, blending, chopping, grating, steaming.

They want to see her sautéeing, frying, boiling, bleaching, baking, simmering, cooking, poaching.

She should be sorting, folding, washing, bleaching, ironing.

She should have the crockpot at her table in court, making tonite's dinner, excited about this month's low-fat recipes, or she should be embroidering her children's pillowcases.

She should be getting ready for Christmas, hand-whittling wooden tops, volunteering at the junior league, crocheting sun hats.

She should have her children's pictures with her at all times.

Whenever a mother does something for herself, it's taken as something she is not doing for her child.

AMERICAN CHESTNUT

WHEN NICKY GOT to the party, her grandmother was blowing out the candles. Then Lily stood up to make a speech. We have something else to celebrate tonight. A miracle has happened. The American chestnut has bloomed for the first time in over 75 years! You see, the American chestnut was once the most common tree in America. But a blight wiped out nearly every tree. This tree has survived. The disease causes the tree to never mature, but to continually send up new shoots, trying to survive. This is a very special accomplishment for this tree, to be able to bloom. Let us cut the cake.

Later, at the party, Mr. Dove, Beatrice, and Lily and other people stood around the tree, patting it fondly for a job well done. Nicky could hear the conversation. "Sometimes if you keep trying, you just might bloom, even at our age." Beatrice, Mr. Dove, and Lily laughed. A warm wind swept through the tree and made a beautiful sound.

MONTECITO

I AM IN Montecito vacationing and it all comes back to me—how, some fifteen years ago, I was picked up by two men delivering mattresses, and how they tried to rape me. I outsmarted them. I said "I can't go down on you in the front seat—your dick is so big—I could give you better head in the back—your dick is so big." Nothing makes a man feel better than telling him his dick is big. I pretended like I liked him 'cause I could tell, in my teenage way, that no one had ever liked him. They were watching me as I got out of the truck, and I said "Let's move the mattresses next to each other on the floor, then I can suck you and your friend can fuck me or I can work you both with my hands." The mattresses were heavy and it took the two of them. I pretended to help, but then I ran. I ran, I ran. Oh yes, I ran. We were stopped in Montecito, in a parking lot overlooking the ocean, and there were stores above, on a hill, and I ran and ran til I got to that store—got to an entrance. Got to get to the entrance—You see I ain't got nothing—

I ain't got money, a car, a degree—I ain't got nothing but me.

They think they can have me 'cause they are stronger than me.

All I got is wits.

All I got is wits.

I look at all the wealth. The big houses that overlook water, with domestics, where every spill is cleaned up by someone else—where everything is priceless and no one smells bad.

I'm still running and they are getting in their truck. Maybe they'll catch me. I hate myself for being a girl. For being young. For this costume of heels and makeup, of earrings that get caught. I'm dressed for the occasion—the occasion of being female. Being caught female. If I ever have a daughter I must teach her of this moment in a woman's life, of running. Running. Running. Caught. I'm caught.

"You should have run faster." All of the penguins had to be kept inside, since people had been known to shoot and stab them.

"Why don't you fight back?" And I answer to myself, the sheep have more than one stomach and if they fall in a certain way their stomachs get all tangled up, they can't get up, and they can die.

"I know you're bleeding profusely but I need to see some identification before I file a report." All of the animals at the children's zoo had extensive bruising to their vulvas and anuses, perhaps from the insertion of a blunt object.

I'm back here fifteen years later, and today I want to talk to God, but the only one he sends me is Jack Kerouac, and so I tell Jack, "That *On The Road* stuff almost got me killed. I don't have the privilege of going on the road, as a woman, as a mother. You glorify your irresponsibility—I bet you were the worst father in the world. You were just some drunken guy."

Then God sends me William Burroughs. "You are no hero to me. You shot your wife—yeah, a big artsy guy. You are no god to me."

I felt better but then I said to God, "You make life tough—you make life hard."

Then I got hit by a car but I was crying, I was so happy, cause those mattress goons weren't taking me away. For now, I'm safe, and if I'm lucky my face might be smashed up and then I'll really be free. I'll really be free.

Yes, I'm lucky.

This morning the black walnut began to shed its leaves.

THE END

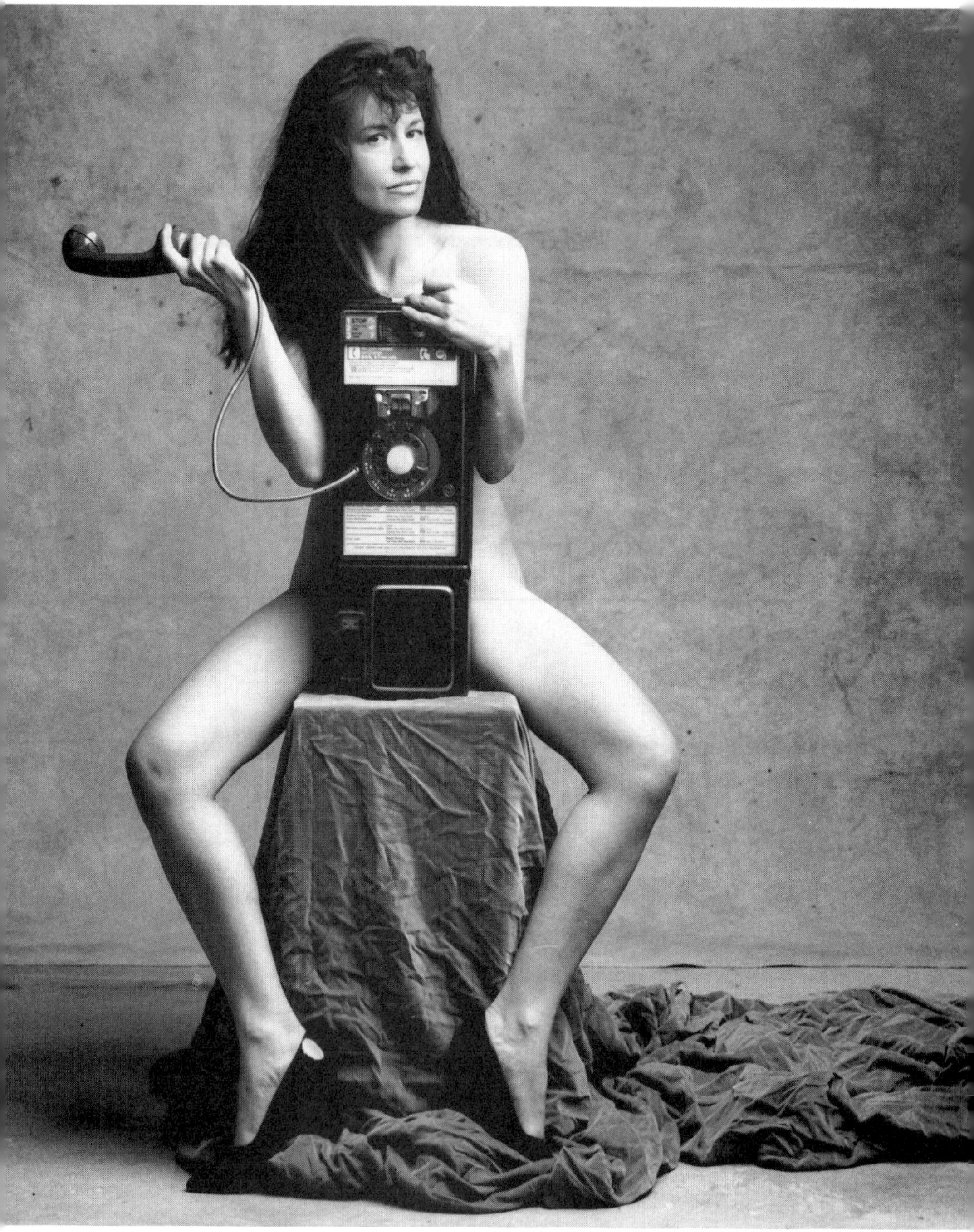

I N 1997, MOCA curators Julie Lazar and Tom Finkelspearl began commissioning work for an exhibition of "public art." The art that was created for this exhibition was fascinating in its scope. Mel Chin, for example, worked with California Institute of Art students to create artworks for the set of *Melrose Place*. After being used on the show, the artworks—

20

UNCOMMON SENSE

sheets, pictures, and other objects—were displayed at MOCA and later auctioned. Rick Lowe created a housing project out of an abandoned house in Watts. Creating housing was his art form.

I was approached to participate in the show, and I decided that my public work would take the form of a 900 number. I was so often accused of being obscene or indecent that I thought it would be fitting to place myself within the 1-900-FANTASY sex-call milieu.

The piece wound up not working out for the MOCA show, but I did the project—1-900-ALL-KAREN—with Creative Time in 1998. I performed for six months, with a new performance in the form of a short pre-recorded phone message each day. I would talk about the Supreme Court, perform excerpts from my repertoire, etc. And yes, people paid by the minute to hear me, and they could leave messages that I would listen to.

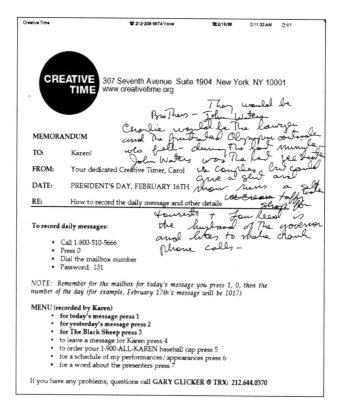

Creative Time · ☎ 212-206-6674 Voice · 📅 2/16/98 · 🕚 11:33 AM · 📄 1/1

CREATIVE TIME
307 Seventh Avenue Suite 1904 New York, NY 10001
www.creativetime.org

MEMORANDUM

TO: Karen!

FROM: Your dedicated Creative Timer, Carol

DATE: PRESIDENT'S DAY, FEBRUARY 16TH

RE: How to record the daily message and other details

To record daily messages:

- Call 1-800-510-5666
- Press 0
- Dial the mailbox number
- Password: 131

NOTE: Remember for the mailbox for today's message you press 1, 0, then the number of the day (for example, February 17th's message will be 1017)

MENU (recorded by Karen)

- for today's message press 1
- for yesterday's message press 2
- for The Black Sheep press 3
- to leave a message for Karen press 4
- to order your 1-900-ALL-KAREN baseball cap press 5
- for a schedule of my performances / appearances press 6
- for a word about the presenters press 7

If you have any problems, questions call **GARY GLICKER @ TRX: 212.644.0370**

Last nite il saw the new Lou Reed documentary)
it was fab –
2 nites ago il met Lou Reed
and hung out with Charlie Rose + John Waters
and To'nite il got my period. I'd love to see
those 3 in a sitcom together – as Playboys
Last nite il saw a friend who was born
a man who il knew as a woman and
now

I was preoccupied with the notion that the artist should be respected as a professional. I wanted people to recognize that the education and seriousness that goes into being an arts professional is similar to the preparation required for other professions. I was hoping to make the point that, if I really wanted to be obscene and sexually exploitative, I could have been doing porn all along and making a lot more money. All the artists could. But I wasn't a porn star—I was a trained artist.

After doing the 1-900 piece, I became interested in showing the learning process of the visual artist. I wanted to put the studio, the classroom, into the museum setting.

My piece "Go Figure" is a classroom studio. Easels and art supplies are available to the public, and a nude model poses on a dais. People who come to the museum are put in the position of artist by being given a chance to draw the nude. What I liked best was that the drawings were hung up in the studio, so anyone who participated in the piece could say that their work was hanging in a museum.

Alongside "Go Figure," I mounted an installation involving two terra-cotta reproductions of Greek statues, a female and a male. I videotaped phallic and vulvic images that were projected onto the statues over the genital areas. On the male I had a banana, ballet slip-

LYLE ASHTON HARRIS, COURTESY OF LOS ANGELES MUSEUM OF CONTEMPORARY ART

LYLE ASHTON HARRIS, COURTESY OF LOS ANGELES MUSEUM OF CONTEMPORARY ART

A DIFFERENT KIND OF INTIMACY

and a cigar projected onto the groin. And on the female I had jelly-fish, an oyster, and a woman slipping her tongue through her lips, projected sideways so it looked like a labia. The installation was dark, with the room painted blue, and there were garden benches, trellises, and flowers. In the back of the statues was a fountain.

There was a computer in the room, with the "Fear of Offending" website onscreen. An image of the website was projected onto the fountain. The website asked visitors what they found offensive. People could type in their answers, and their words would be projected onto the water in the fountain, so that the text appeared to be floating there.

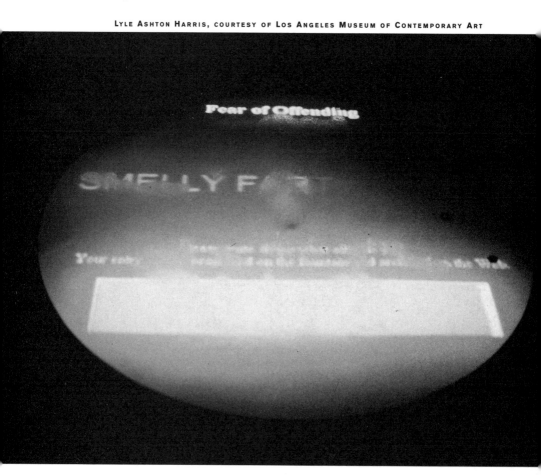

The "Go Figure/Fear of Offending" show was called *Uncommon Sense*. Before the opening, there was concern about the nudity in the classroom and about potentially obscene text appearing on the Web, and whether the darkness of the exhibit might encourage men to surreptitiously masturbate. The fact that my biggest supporters would need to be thinking about every sexual innuendo in the work in order to outguess potential lawsuits was the reality of musem programming.

I had edited the video used in the show at a porn studio, because the editor was very good friends with one of the museum staff members. So there were people from the porn world at the opening. A debate began at the opening, carried on via the website, over what the definition of obscenity should be. Some off-color words were definitely used. But in the end, nobody got sued. There were no problems. And no one was caught masturbating.

VIOLET WAS TWO. As a mother, I was being inundated by mass-marketed children's books, movies and toys. I was struck by the fact that, except for Barbie of course, there were practically no female characters in these fictional worlds. Even within the liberal context of PBS programming, there were no significant female characters. In Disney movies, the animated female characters always seemed to attain happiness via their quest for a man. Even in the liberal-sanctioned Winnie the Pooh, the only female is Kanga—the mother. The reason for this disparity is that girls can look up to male characters but boys can't look up to a female character. Barney is a boy. Big Bird is a boy. Etc., etc.

In my little hamlet of Nyack, Winnie the Pooh was very popular among parents of young children. One night my daughter couldn't sleep and we watched a Pooh video. While watching, I started imagining a whole new subtext. I imagined that the entire cast was gay. I pictured Winnie in chaps. I imagined them with all kinds of psychological problems: Eeyore depressed, Pooh with an eating disorder. In addition to incorporating these ideas into *American Chestnut*, I also started doing drawings, in the style of the original Pooh illustrations, and once I started I couldn't stop. I created some fifty drawings. They were exhibited as part of *Uncommon Sense*.

After the exhibition I realized that the drawings had to be made into a book. I contacted Distributed Art Publishers, a leading distributor of art books, and they put me in contact with Susan Martin from Smart Art Press in L.A. Tom Patchett, the publisher, is a tremendous comedy writer and he inspired me to take the parody farther—to show Pooh selling out to Disney.

The distributor, DAP, bowed out. Along with Barnes and Noble, they were involved in a lawsuit over the distribution of Sally Mann's and Jock Sturges's books, which the right-wing arbiters of family values, with their usual intelligence and taste, had declared "child pornography." DAP could not handle another potential lawsuit with my book. The fear of lawsuits seemed to have pervaded the entire publishing industry. Lawyers told Tom that he shouldn't do Pooh—that Disney, who owned the rights to the characters, would sue—but he persevered. The book was eventually published in 1999 with the legal guidance of Ed Degrazia, who had handled many publishing-related legal situations, including *Naked Lunch* and *Tropic Of Cancer*.

from **Pooh Unplugged**

a parody

the psychological profile of 100 Acre Woool

WINNIE the pooh — eating disorder

Eeyore - flat-out depressed

Tigger — manic depressed

Piglet — low self esteem

Kanga + Roo — oedipus thing

Rabbit — passive aggressive

OWL — delusions of grandeur

OWL IS GREAT

Christopher Robin — the enabler

"Please spank me first, Pooh," quipped Pig[
"and Rabbit and Tigger can pee on me".

I just have to put my mask on then we're ready.

It's Eisner

I don't care what you pay me, Mike....
I won't do any spinoff that involves
MUD BATHS or any of that wee wee wee all the way
home crap.

This must be what they meant by a
7 figure deal with gross participation in the
back end ..

So we don't have anywhere
to spend the Disney money
but we can pretend —

I N 1993, WE won our case in the ninth circuit in Los Angeles. Our grants were reinstated and we were awarded $252,000. Most went to the attorneys. Each plaintiff got a few thousand dollars. I got my grant and then $2,000 for damages.

In the fall of 1996 I toured *American Chestnut* in support of my book *Living It*

21

SUPREME COURT

Up. My first stop on the tour was Portland, Oregon. I was traveling with my mother and daughter. I was scheduled to start doing interviews right away and the first one happened when I got to the hotel. The journalist was kind, courteous and professional. The interview went well, until she asked her first question about the NEA. She asked me if the case had helped my career. I froze up. Suddenly my voice became tense and hoarse and I couldn't talk. Later on, it got worse. I had physically and psychologically lost my voice.

I had to cancel the tour. I decided that I needed to use the illness as an opportunity: I would use the physical illness to uncover the real sickness. I realized that my physical illness had started with my psychic inability to answer questions about the NEA. I had lost my voice in regard to the issue. I could no longer handle the stress of the case, emotionally or physically.

The strain was showing in my marriage. Michael and I separated in 1997. It seemed like I was losing so much, even the ability to cope with the events in my life.

The Clinton administration could have let the decision of the Ninth Circuit stand, but they didn't. They appealed the decision. Their goal was to overturn the ninth Circuit's ruling that the decency clause was unconstitutional, thereby allowing the amendment to remain on the books. I believe that Clinton was using the NEA as a bargaining chip for gaining leverage with the right. If he went along with the right's point of view and appealed the decision, there would be nothing the Republicans could do to him. The issue would become a moot point as far as he was concerned.

So the "liberal" Bill Clinton—not a Republican, not a Christian far-right extremist—was responsible for bringing the case to the Supreme Court, where we would eventually lose.

IT HAD BEEN nearly eight years since the court case began. But the date for the Supreme Court to hear the arguments had finally arrived.

I flew to Washington DC to hear the Supreme Court arguments. It was a beautiful day in March 1998. Two of my fellow plaintiffs, Holly and Tim, were present. Holly has a fantastic sense of humor and she was making remarks that were keeping me in the moment. Other arts organizations and arts supporters from around the country were there as well. I looked around at all the artists, journalists, and art organizers and realized how many people had been involved in championing us and the arts.

The visual presentation of the Supreme Court is meant to recall Mount Olympus: the steps leading up to the Court; the Ionic columns; the justices in their robes. It was more like being on a cheesy movie set than in a court of law, and the moment felt more surreal than momentous. I looked at the platform where the justices were seated and I felt sickened by the hokiness of it—costuming and presenting these public officials as if they were Greek gods.

David Cole did the arguing. He of course did an excellent job— he and the other atttorneys who had worked so hard and so dilligently for this moment. What amazed me was how little the justices seemed to know of the case, of us, of the consequences their decision would have. It was as if they were hearing it all for the first time. When it was over, I had a feeling we weren't going to win.

On the steps of the court the plaintiffs gave their takes on the day. What came out of my mouth surprised me. I said that I felt that Jesse Helms had been sexually harassing me—that he had taken my profession, my career, and had eroticized me and my work. I felt I had been embroiled in an abusive, public sexual relationship with Helms and the far right. He made me into a battered woman, if only psychologically. If I had realized all of this before, I would have sued Mr. Helms for sexual harassment.

1

(10:17 a.m.)

2

CHIEF JUSTICE REHNQUIST: We'll hear argument

3

first this morning in Number 97-371, National Endowment

4

for the Arts v. Karen Finley.

5

General Waxman.

6

ORAL ARGUMENT OF SETH P. WAXMAN

7

ON BEHALF OF THE PETITIONERS

8

GENERAL WAXMAN: Mr. Chief Justice, and may it

9

please the Court:

10

Since 1965, the National Endowment for the Arts

11

has selectively provided funding, public funding to arts

12

projects on the basis of aesthetic judgments in order to

13

enrich the lives of all Americans and to expand public

14

appreciation of art.

15

The question presented in this case is whether,

16

although it thus expands the opportunities for artistic

17

expression, Congress violated the First Amendment -- that

18

is, made a law abridging the freedom of speech -- by

19

directing that the NEA ensure, quote, that artistic

20

excellence and artistic merit are the standards by which

21

applications are judged, taking into consideration general

22

standards of decency and respect for the diverse beliefs

23

and values of the American public.

24

25

3

ALDERSON REPORTING COMPANY, INC.
1111 FOURTEENTH STREET, N.W.
SUITE 400
WASHINGTON, D.C. 20005
(202)289-2260
(800) FOR DEPO

I HAD HAD MY deposition for the NEA case in the spring of 1993. It took two days. I was almost eight months pregnant by then. The deposition took place in Mary Dorman's office in New York. The questioning was ridiculous. The NEA's attorneys acted as if they thought that, if they were crafty enough, they'd get me to accidentally admit that my work was

22

THE RETURN OF THE CHOCOLATE-SMEARED WOMAN

"obscene." They constantly referred to the "sexual" elements of the piece, to body parts, to the food. There was an erotic element in the questioning. "Ms. Finley, did you ever touch a breast while performing? Did you care if you were looked at by men?" And on and on. After hours of this I couldn't take it anymore, and I accused the attorney who was questioning me of being like Roy Cohn. I felt like I was being questioned as if I was a Communist during the Red Scare. I said, "You sound like you're getting a little too into this." This attorney later asked my attorney, in my presence, to assure him that I wouldn't transform his questioning into an artwork. I think that's when the seed of the idea that eventually became *The Return of the Chocolate-Smeared Woman* was planted.

Although the Supreme Court hearing was in March 1998, a decision was not to be expected until July. In the meantime, I decided to deconstruct my own performance, *We Keep Our Victims Ready*, which in a sense had started it all. I decided to incorporate autobiographical elements that had to do with the case, as well. I expanded on the premise that Jesse Helms had initiated a public, sexually abusive relationship with me. I went further with the concept by acknowledging that I was complicit in the dynamic.

That realization occured to me as a result of appearing on *Politically Incorrect*. But it wasn't hashing out the issues in front of the studio audience that brought on this insight—it was having my underpants stolen.

I had first appeared on the show in spring 1997 and had been on several times since then. For one appearance, I was booked into a hotel in Japan Town where I stayed the night before the taping. On the day of the show, someone broke into my room while I was out and stole my underwear and stockings and bras. I was very upset. I had bought a minidress that needed a particular pair of underpants and stockings to wear on the show.

The hotel catered to Japanese tourists. When I called downstairs to tell them what had happened, the person on the other end couldn't understand my English. So I ran downstairs in my mini dress and gesticulated wildly at the concierge, trying to make him understand what had happened. Standing there half-dressed, I must have looked like a prostitute. I'm sure it gave the hotel a nice pay-by-the-hour ambience.

I raised my voice, as if that would make it easier for the staff to understand me. "SOMEONE TOOK MY PANTIES!" But no one could figure out what I was talking about, so they ignored me.

I needed to get to the studio and I had no underwear, stockings or bra. So on the way, the limo driver had to pull up in front of Macy's at Beverly Center so I could run in and buy undies. I felt like I was in a sitcom.

The experience actually helped me. It made me feel so exposed that I thought, the hell with it. My privacy had been literally stripped away. I no longer felt the need to be emotionally on the defensive. While discussing the Monica–Bill affair with Bill Maher and the rest of the panel, I gave my opinion that this affair was part of Bill and Hillary's erotic dynamic. Her humiliation, his need to be forgiven, her need to stand by his side. They both get off on it.

Since I was tinkering with the idea of my own kinky relationship with Jesse Helms it was natural for me to apply this idea to my own story. The realization that I was not just a passive object in the relationship was a positive one, because it made me realize I had an option. I could act, not just react. I decided to end my relationship with Jesse Helms, and to get out of the role of victim once and for all. I would reclaim control of my art, my expression. *The Return of the Chocolate-Smeared Woman* took shape over the next couple of months.

Theater director Jim Simpson had recently opened the Bat Theatre where the Millenium, a TriBeCa space that showed experimental film, had once been. I met with Jim and we decided to work together.

The theater was under construction while we were rehearsing. Since the space was small, the stage surrounded 3/4 of the room. There wasn't time to put in seats, so the audience sat on overturned buckets.

Jim had put together a dance troupe who were to be painted in chocolate. The performance started with the troupe go-go dancing on a sixties-style set, with their hair done up in flips and bouffants, naked except for their underwear, and smeared with chocolate. Then I smeared myself with chocolate and joined them. Instead of the chocolate representing the humiliation of the past, I now wanted to play it up as an erotic element. I invited the audience to lick the chocolate off my body for twenty dollars.

The performance was very camp. I did redo "Why Can't This Veal Calf Walk?" with a Greek chorus of chocolate women. But I also included tales of lust between me and politicians, and other bawdy material. By embracing the deviant character that the right had imposed on me, I felt I was in control. I no longer needed to defend or explain.

DONA ANN MCADAMS

A DIFFERENT KIND OF INTIMACY

from ***The Return of the Chocolate-Smeared Woman***

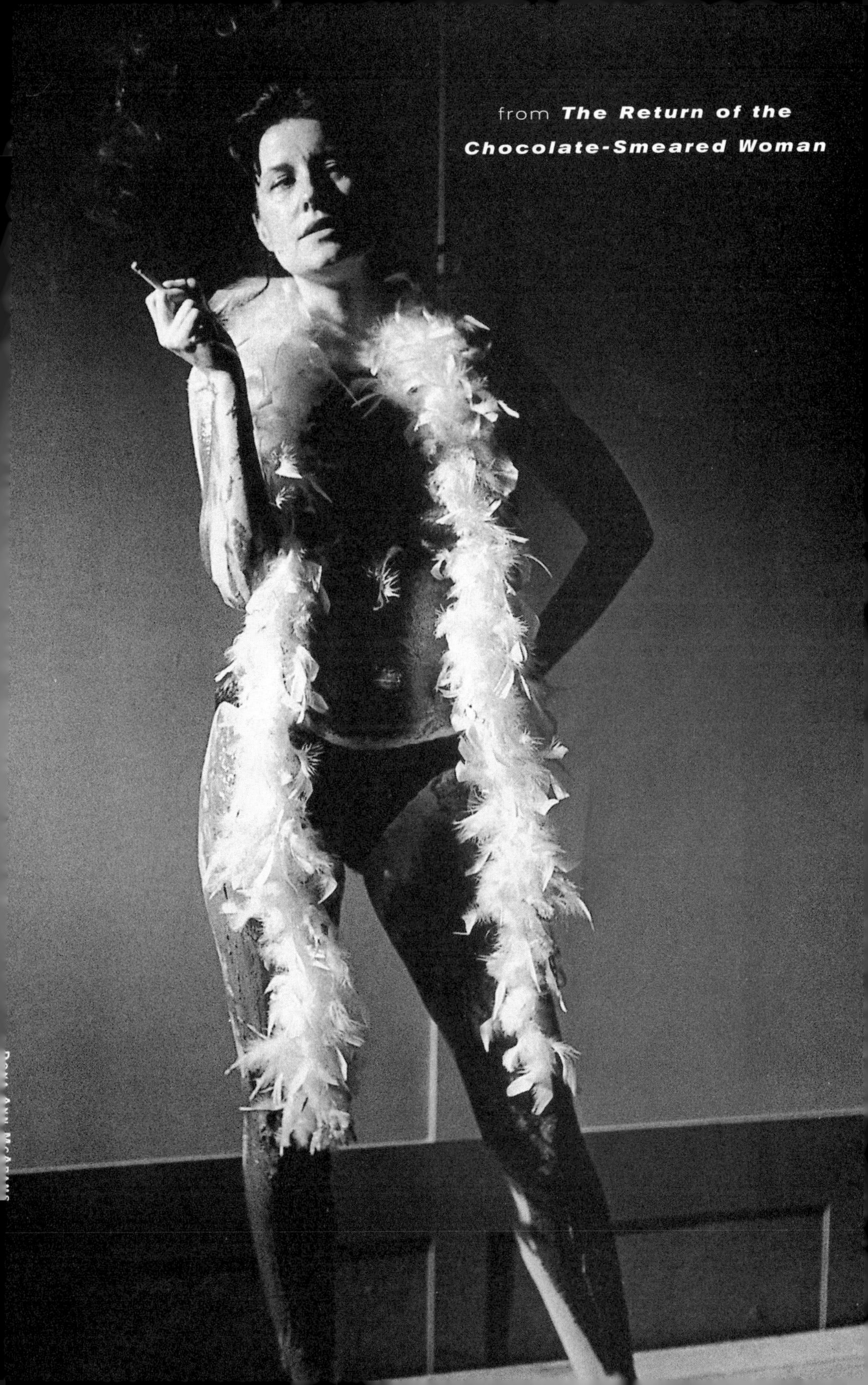

I'VE COME TO realize that I've been in an eight-year, sexually abusive relationship with Jesse Helms. Jesse is intensely, erotically, passionately out of control in his sexual need to dominate me. And I've had enough. The sexual relationship began on the Senate floor, when he eroticized my career, my work, my livelihood. He could never just see me as a person doing my job. Jesse just always gets an erection when my name is mentioned. He masturbates to visions of my body smeared in chocolate while looking at my picture, and he gets himself in a frenzy publicly humiliating me. "She, she, she, is filthy. She is disgusting, this vile wicked creature with chocolate on her naked breasts, you obscene, indecent creature, writhing, wwrrrriitthing naked on stage, paid for by taxpayer money," and I respond while lying in bed, waiting for my southern gentleman. I look at Jesse and I say "Lick it off of me, Jesse. Lick me. Gum me. Gum me you, you old conservative cooter."

I get off in this relationship. Sometimes I defend myself. I put all of my energy into showing him I'm a good girl. "Jesse, I'm just a working girl. I have a Masters degree, a Guggenheim. Lectured at Yale, Harvard." But it doesn't work. He just goes further and further in degrading me, humiliating me, til I become an abused woman on the job. And today I'm telling you, I'm out of this relationship. Do you think I ever got off in this relationship? Jesse did. I get off in my own way.

It almost killed Jesse when he heard that Clinton was sticking his dick out at me all the time. Now, you're wondering how I got connected with Bill. Or as I call him, Willy. Easy. Chelsea was doing my monologues in the basement of the White House. And Bill thought I'd understand his problem. So, I'd say, "Jesse, you can do that too. Jesse, you can stick your dick out at me."

Clinton is always calling me. "Meet me at this gas station on Highway 66. Meet me at the restroom at the UN," to suck his dick. And you know what I would say to Bill? I'd say "BILL, I WANT YOU TO FUCK ME!" and hang up. Bill won't fuck me. We do everything else.

See, actually, Jesse likes me from behind. I don't like taking it in the ass. But I'll do it for Jesse. It thrills him. He'd say, "Chocolate bitch, I'm going to fuck your little butt." And I'd go, "No, No, you're not." Then we'd fight, make up. I love

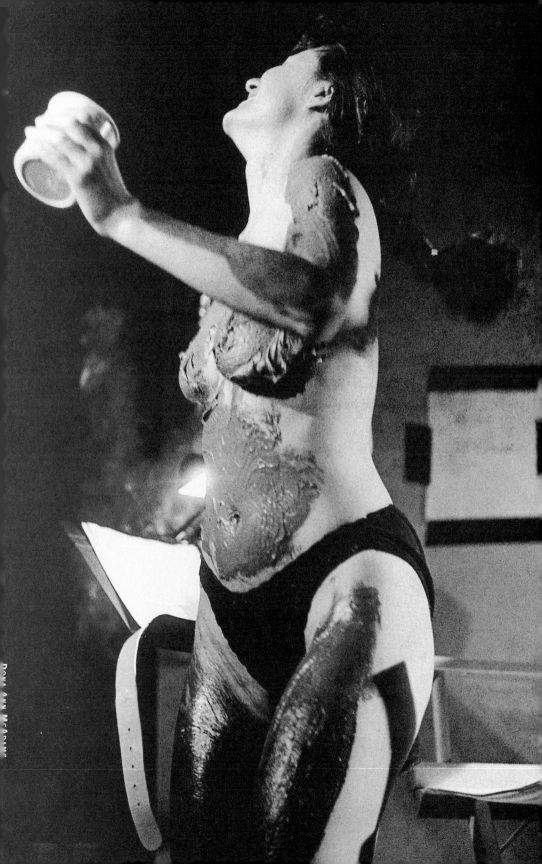

making up. But I'm so fucking sick of chocolate. He loved it when I'd give him a cocoa crispie. That is when I'd wank Jesse off in hot, steaming chocolate, really slow. He really wanted it to be shit. I think he does have an obsession with the asshole. So while I'm wanking him, I call him asshole, dirty, old, wrinkly butthole.

Now, the power play is that Newt Gingrich is just waiting for me. He said as soon as Jesse is finished with me then I'd have him. "Oh, God," I said, "I'm not going to scream out Newt, Newt when I'm coming." I said, "You don't have to leave your wife, but change your name."

Newt asked me what I needed, what he could do for me. And I said, "I need my house cleaned. And I want you to do it." So, I masturbate, file my nails, doing what girls do, while Newt is licking my toilet bowl clean. Yeah, he wants me sososo soso bad. Then while he's licking my piss, shit, and blood out of the toilet, Clinton calls my machine.

"This is the presidential dick calling. This is the chief of state cock calling. This the cock of the nation. It's all yours, baby. It's all yours, my yammy mammy."

Oh, does this make Newt mad. Newt is furious. I go "Yeah, your dick is not good enough, Newt." I say, "No one wants your dick. Every woman wants the power dick." And Jesse, you are are no longer fucking with me.

* * *

THE RETURN OF the *Chocolate-Smeared Woman* ran for a month in the summer of 1998. During that time, the Court's decision was handed down. We lost. The government was going to be allowed to place restrictions on funding based on value judgments.

When I heard the decision, I decided to hold a press conference instead of doing my usual performance. I sat onstage at the Bat Theater with microphone in hand, fielding questions, my body covered in chocolate. I was inspired by Abbie Hoffman's sensibility; I wanted to turn the bad news into a performance on my turf. Most of the journalists seemed to understand the surreal and tongue-in-cheek aspect of it all.

That night, someone sent a dozen roses to me at the theater. The card read, "The show is not over until the chocolate woman sings." It was signed, "An anonymous Souter." If this was really a card from David Souter—the only Justice to vote on our behalf—I will never know. But I keep the card in my linen closet, where I can look at it whenever I grab a towel to go sing in the shower.

THERE WAS GOING to be a show on the nude at the Whitney in late 1998, and I was to be included. I was planning on recreating *Go Figure* and performing nude in short segments at various locations throughout the museum. Five days after the case was lost, I was told that the show had been cancelled for lack of funding. When the *New York Times* heard of this, they reported on it with interest, saying that the Whitney cancelling a show for lack of funding, particularly so close to the opening date, was unusual. I later mounted the piece at the Aldrich Museum in Connecticut.

I had other premieres and shows in the works at other New York institutions, and many of these institutions closed their doors on me. People with whom I had been in dialogue stopped returning my phone calls.

A few weeks after the case was lost and the show at the Whitney was cancelled, my mother started bringing me books on women who had been censored or who had incorporated sexuality into their work. I read biographies and historical accounts of Mae West and Josephine Baker.

One day my mother and I went to a used bookstore, where my mother found the book *Through The Flower* by Judy Chicago. Although I had read the book previously, I reread it then. In the book, Judy talks about how, after the *Dinner Party*, she became depressed and withdrawn because of the critical reactions to her work. Reading about her emotional process helped me to find a process appropriate for me. Hearing about her experiences with censorship and her battles for recognition, I gained a perspective I needed.

Soon after, I went to Michigan for the Women's Music Festival. This music festival, which hosts only women, has thousands of visitors. It is a woman's Woodstock, so to speak, with performances, music, dancing.

After the performance I went to have some food at the mess tent. I sat at a table with a few women and one woman struck up a conversation with me, telling me that she liked my performance. We started talking about censorship, Josephine Baker, and the dangers of portraying women's sexuality. We began to talk about archetypes and the notion of transformation: the idea that people embody different archetypes at different times, and that now might be the time for me to transform from one archetype—the Hero-Martyr—to another. I actually felt for a moment that it was a divine intervention for me to be talking to this woman because what she was saying was so revelatory to me. Then she was called by name to come up to the front and I realized that I was speaking with Alice Walker.

VIOLET AND MY mother, Mary, accompanied me to Chicago for a performance. Mary had been living with me in Nyack. She was a great friend to me and her support was particularly important during that time. We were very close.

Mary wasn't feeling well in Chicago. She had a nagging cold. From Chicago we went to Iowa, and there, my mother started coughing up blood. We returned home and I took my mother to the doctor and she had a chest x-ray.

Three months after the court decision, my mother was diagnosed with lung cancer. Several months later, she moved back to Chicago to be with the rest of my family.

My mother died in my arms. It was in the same hospital where my grandmother had died, the same hospital where my mother gave birth to my brother Brian. The hospital was just down the street from where we all lived. A few blocks from where my father committed suicide. I couldn't go to my mother's funeral, I just couldn't.

T WAS JOHN WATERS who helped bring the feeling of joy — the joy of performing — back into my life. While in Atlanta, performing at the Seven Stages Theatre, I was invited to go to a dinner for him. His photos were included in an AIDS benefit taking place there.

One of the photos was called "Twelve Assholes and a Dirty Shoe." And that is

23

HEALING HOLLYWOOD STYLE

exactly what it was a picture of—twelve assholes and a dirty shoe. It was presented with a red velvet curtain as a frame. When I looked at it I started to laugh out loud. I just couldn't stop. It came out of an uncontrollable place in me. I was breaking a taboo—laughing at an AIDS benefit.

Up until then I had dealt with the crisis and sadness of AIDS by making art that paralleled the emotions of the crisis. John's work— the idea of bringing the assholes into view without apology for the humour and absurdity of it—was liberating for me. Within one day my attitude changed. I went to Saks to shop. I opened a charge card right there and spent 700 dollars I didn't have on clothes I didn't need. I bought a pair of blue tiger-print Moschino pants and a big fluffy coat. I had my hair done and I was a different person.

I got the Hollywood bug. I had just returned from a trip to L.A. to go to a party for my 900 number at the Thomas Healy Gallery in Chelsea. I had cocktails with John Waters, who instructed me to smile and be nice to the FOX television crew. Charlie Rose was at the post-opening dinner. And then I had coffee and desert with Lou Reed. Instead of being downtown blasé about it all, I spent the evening fantasizing about the three men as brothers in a sitcom. They inherit a taffy business on the boardwalk in Atlantic City.

I couldn't stand being the Joan of Arc of the art world anymore. Internally, I was burning at the stake from the constant battles of defending the first amendment. The icon of free speech was becoming a pile of ashes.

I had to rethink my career, my persona, my work. I needed an archetype makeover. So I started an unravelling process that involved geographical shifts.

My whole heroic complex, I decided, was enabled by my relationship with New York City, because New York is so self-important. I looked at New York and fell out of love. I was becoming annoyed with all of the city's idiosyncracies, the way you suddenly become annoyed with the idiosyncracies of a soon-to-be-ex-lover. I was tired of the survivor mentality of New York, the way everybody is so proud of their stamina, of the fact that they can brave the subway crowds and stay out all night and wear nothing but black for ten years straight. Most of all, I was tired of all that history. I couldn't look at anything old. I couldn't look at the thing I had once loved, New York City. So, on the rebound, I turned to a new lover, a new relationship: Los Angeles.

I threw out 57 Hefty trash bags of art supplies and closed my studio. Anything that I had made that was associated with the court case, I threw out.

I got an apartment in Los Angeles via fax.

I posed sexily, covered in chocolate, for a photo that appeared in *Time*. The photo was spotted by Marilyn Grabowski, an editor at *Playboy*'s Santa Monica office. I found myself in a conversation with her in her office. Talking to her about sexual politics with a photo of Pamela Anderson in the background satisfied me in a way that talking to artworld intellectuals never had.

It seemed so perfect that I had been named a woman of the year by *Ms.* and would now be posing for *Playboy*. And I would be posing in chocolate, which for eight years I had been insisting was not a sexual symbol at all. My enemies had eroticized me against my will, so this was like taking control and ending things myself. It was a way of saying "Case Closed" — and getting the last word.

The *Playboy* Studios were truly inspirational. The larger-than-life photographs of Playmates posing on all kinds of surreal "sets" looked ready to go straight into the Whitney Biennial. I went to the set designer and told him that I would need three sets for my shoot. The first was a western look, with lots of phallic cacti and guns in holsters. The second was an outer space look, with alien/astronaut foreplay against a lunar landscape. And the third was an igloo. The *Playboy* staff didn't share my vision. I was given one set: a bed, tastefully made up with chocolate-colored sheets.

The *Playboy* Studios bathrooms use toilets as rotating super-bidets—an effective shower for your private parts—which the models use before their shoots. As I sat on one of these, I felt like I was in a pornographic Esther Williams musical, and I laughed. Finally, I wasn't taking myself so seriously.

A DIFFERENT KIND OF INTIMACY

But the academic in me was still there. I just had to ask the woman grooming my muff, "What do you go for in creating a good muff look?" Answer: "A youthful-looking muff." She streaked my feminine hair with a copper tint. When I joked about this, she told me, "This is my profession and I take it seriously."

I posed dripping Hershey's chocolate onto my breasts. The photographer told me I wasn't posing in a *Playboy*-sexy way. I raised my voice. "I'm standing here naked in four-inch heels dripping chocolate on my breasts. THIS IS SEXY!"

NOW THAT I was situated in L.A. I was invited to speak with a Hollywood agent. I had been reluctant to do this, but somebody had told me that this agent was "sensitive" and would "understand" me. The conversation went something like this:

"Ms. Finley, I love the female voice. I've known Sandra—and I must tell you, before I go on with any of your ideas, that I have a project here at the agency that has been waiting for you. A project that has been waiting to be filled for the last twenty years. Whoopi turned it down—but I think you could do the project justice. What we would first like to propose to do with you is the new, female Animal House. Now, it is a no-brainer, Ms. Finley. Lots of young, nubile sorority women of different colors, for multicultural diversity, and—well, you, Ms. Finley, would be in charge of the sorority and there would be a food fight—sloppy joe, corn, mashed potatos, peas, all dripping from young naked students. And with your background of food and the body—like I said, it is a no-brainer.

"Now, while that is in the can, Ms. Finley, I'd like to do a buddy film with the likes of Bette Midler. Since she is married to a performance artist. You, the controversial artist, stuck at borders in third world countries—espionage, intrigue. Now the angle, the laugh line, is going to be you going through customs and the agents going through your props and you will be explaining your props. And they ask, 'You put this in what orifice?'

"And then, something I have gotten a start on is your very own miniseries that I think we could get HBO going on immediately. *The Karen Finley Story*. Your legal and censorship battles."

"Oh, I'd like that," I replied. "It could center on the drama of the case personally and publicly—the death threats, my miscarriage, the politicians, Ollie North, the president, Helms."

"Oh, no, we're not interested in that," said the sensitive agent.

"Well, then, you'll focus on the actual Supreme Court case and decision," I surmised.

"No, the Supreme Court will merely be a backdrop, like the bar in *Cheers*," he gloated.

I tried to be interested and positive. "Well," I said, "what else is there?"

"Why, Ms. Finley, you look so good in clothes!," he segued abruptly. "Mary Tyler Moore. Candace Bergen. Marlo Thomas. It's all about the look. It's all about clothes."

I WAS TEACHING at the California Institute of the Arts when I first moved to L.A. After I'd been there several months, the dean asked me to attend a meeting about a drawing by two students from the department. The drawing was causing an uproar; it was a parody depicting faculty, staff, and students in an orgy. It was exhibited for critique. An 82-year-old staff member was depicted in the drawing, and when somebody showed it to her, she went to the hospital in a state of trauma. She never returned to her job, and the school is currently being sued.

At the meeting it was decided that there should be an open forum for the matter to be discussed. I merely sat quietly during the forum, refraining from an oratory rant on the importance of free speech. I didn't feel the need to be the voice of justice.

Perhaps this is all self-censorship, but I feel it is a shift away from self-righteous self-involvement. Now I'm interested in post-feminist self-involvement: Hair and Nails.

I was an honored guest at a publishing party given for the *Nation* magazine in New York. I chatted with one of the magazine's editors, and mentioned that I moved to Hollywood soon after losing the case, and that I was healing nicely, safely away from all New York's integrity. The editor quickly offered her assistance. "We'll set you up with some people of integrity in Los Angeles." But I turned away before she'd finished speaking, for Drew Barrymore's mother had just entered the room.

At the opening of Spa, a night club in New York, I ran into Andres Serrano. I told him I was on sabbatical from the art world and that now I was in the entertainment business. He told me he had a film in him and needed an agent.

I said goodbye and went with Amy Heckerling (*Clueless*) and Stuart Cornfeld (Ben Stiller's producer) to a sake bar before heading back to L.A.

The healing part of show business, I've learned, is that it teaches you that the show must go on.

I had to return to L.A. to be on an episode of *Politically Incorrect* which was to be taped at the Playboy Mansion. On my way to the Playboy game room to get my make-up done, I passed William Shatner on the front steps. Wearing my black lace bustier, I smiled at the camera Hollywood style as I strode arm in arm with Bill Maher. I chatted up Richard Lewis, and then Hugh Hefner joined us in his regalia of silk pajamas. As Bill pointed out, we were at Hugh Hefner's house, and so, after the show, I had to thank him for having me there. I also thanked him for his support of freedom of expression and for his financial contributions to the NEA 4 lawsuit.

As I rolled slowly away in my town car, with the yellow "Playmates at Play" warning sign receding behind me, I remembered talking to Jonathan Demme years ago, when I was consumed with the self-righteousness of my creativity being high art.

It's all entertainment, he told me. And he was right.

*A*FTER I FINISHED *American Chestnut*, I began creating work about arousal, about being turned on.

24

EROTICA

THINK OF ME
WHEN YOU ARE FUCKING HER

They are making love now. I can feel it.

They had dinner and a bottle of wine. They talked and walked. It was raining and the air was chilly, but not cool enough for heat.

I can see her ass as he mounts her—on top of her—

He's groaning, for it's been so long, to have some puss, some pussy meat—and he stops his entrance to kiss her neck—a salty neck—he's pulling at her ear—but he wants to pull at me.

Think of me when you're kissing her.

He reaches down and makes sure she's still there—like the way he left her. Cause the turn-on is only that she listens. The turn on with me is trying to get me to listen. Trying to tame me. And he has to settle into that comfortable position in place.

And he's fucking her, not making love to her, cause he's thinking of me, and he's confused and it gets hotter—It's been too long and really it's not her he's fucking.

Think of me when you are fucking her.

And when you are crying out in orgasm with that hot cum that I made hot I wait for you to remember the one that you said was the best with me. The best with me.

The best with me.

And it just wasn't quite as good with her even though it was tried and true, comfortable like an old pair of jeans,

And after you've cum and after you sleep

and after you relive all the things you did with me

and after you tell her everything you did while you were away

minus me, just brought enough so the jealousy is safe and after you wake up
and do it again

Think of me when you are fucking her

Think of me when you are wanting her

Think of me when you are fucking her.

UGLY MAN

TODAY I WENT into the Radio Shack and saw the ugliest man I'd ever seen. I stared, transfixed by his ugly beauty. His head shaped like a swollen peanut—

Now, I'm not saying swollen penis, although we have all seen our SWOLLEN UGLY PENIS on occasion, and sometimes I just have to say to myself "I'm glad my G-Spot doesn't have eyes."

This ugly man was wearing a tie with a pattern of an eye test. And I thought to myself, "I've got something to work with here other than just looks. I got myself a SMART ugly man." Because for a few moments I'm not looking at his face and I'm looking at that tie with the eye pattern on it. I walked up to him with my tongue licking the inside of my lips—and I took my boot and slowly ran it up his pant leg to his crotch. The other customers stared, for nothing ever happens at the mall.

I brought my finger to his lips and said, "Ugly can be very sexy." A matronly woman in a maroon running outfit came by and said, "I'd love to smell your ass."

A delivery boy said, "I'd love to suck your toes."

The mailman said, "I'd love to rub you down."

And the Ugly cooed and cried and we held him in our arms and sang in the round.

We love you sweet ugly,
We love you our sweet sweet ugly,
We want you ugly,
For being ugly you make us beautiful and for that you are such a dear.

Mercy, I love shopping.

PEDICURE

WHILE HAVING MY pedicure in Denver, the Russian woman took my foot in her hands to massage it. She held my foot firm, almost too firm, and she told me that I would enjoy my massage. Her interest in my foot became luscious, and she told me my foot was perfect as she stroked my arch, maneuvered my foot in slow strolls with skill—and dug her fat knuckles into into into into—

   She grasped the foot and placed it on something soft and she pulled my calf so my heel dug into her breast, then my toes. I resisted, but her arms were strong, and I felt her get more excited at my movement. I decided, what the hell, if my foot that has worked and walked and stood can give a little bit of pleasure—let it. And then I let her take my other foot and do whatever the hell she wanted. And I gave her a twenty when my polish was dry.

I DID A SERIES of art cartoons for the Los Angeles–based magazine *Coagula*, as a reaction to the "proper" art criticism that we see in *Artforum* and *Art in America*.

ART WORLD 25

* ARTIST MAKEOVER *
&◦ FRANK STELLA ◦&

1. **NAME** . CHANGE NAME TO FRANKLY STELLAR

2. **LOCATION** - DO PAINTINGS OF CONSTELLATIONS
   IN NEON AND PLACE ON CEILINGS
   OF TRAIN STATIONS IN FRANCE

3. **CAUSES** - GIVE OUT FRANKLY STELLAR
   tee shirts to WAR ORPHANS IN
   KOSOVO THAT Read MAKE ART NOT WAR

4. **THEORY** GO INTO MUSEUMS AND KNIFE
   YOUR PAINTINGS SAYING
   you always looked at your
   work as time based

5. **COMPETITION** - ~~BECOME~~
   GET A DALMATIAN THAT
   MAKES WEGMAN SQUIRM

6. **Collaboration** - Do a collaboration
   with pettibone AND Patty Smith
   IN CUBA w/ BAM and make
   SURE TO SAY THE IDEA
   WAS ALL YOURS

7. **BeHaviOR** - SHOW UP DRUNK TO ANYTHING

8. FASHION - TAKE YOUR SHIRT OFF AT A TRACK 16 OPENING AND START SCRATCHING ANYTHING HAIRY. Get photo IN LA WEEKLY

9. SEX - MAKE A VIDEO OF HAVING A MENAGÉTOIS w/ KIKI SMITH AND CADY NOLAND WITH A VOICEOVER OF THE GOOD OLD DAYS WITH THEIR DADS.

10. Hollywood - ANYTHING WITH George Lucas But preferably to design The beams from The GUNS for the WEAPONS FOR The NEXT STAR WARS

GOOD LUCK

Karen's Komix / Finley's Funnies
by Karen Finley

How to operate an Art GALLERY AND
THE EXPRESSIONS THAT GO WITH IT

1 — LOOK UP

always look up with disgust and disbelief when someone asks "Is the title UNTITLED or is it Untitled"

2. — TURN AWAY

Turn away when some scraggly ARTIST A LITTLE TOO FAMILIAR COMES TO DROP OFF SLIDES AND HE SAYS HE KNOWS YOUR BROTHER

3.

SMILE casually + walk away from THE DESK WHEN A CRITIC comes in. Stare at Them while They aren't looking

4

When an artist calls more Than TWICE A DAY to see how his/her SNOW is DOING RESpond with I'VE GOT ANOTHER CALL

5. when SOMEONE wants to buy — DROP EVERY THING, STARE IN EYES AND DO WHATEVER IT TAKES, GOSSIP, LIQUOR, EVEN BRING THEM INTO YOUR OFFICE AND GIVE THEM YOUR PRIVATE Number

6. When there is an artist you want — ALWAYS MENTION the C words Collectors, catalogues, critics, color invite, COLOGNE

Karen's Komix / Finley's Funnies
by Karen Finley

Some Thing To Say
When Drawing next to the A

1 I love fucking you but I hear
you work at Pearl Paint. Can you give
me that 30% discount?

2 I'll wear my own condom, thank
and not the one your hand pr...

3 yes the Ed Moses opening was a...
studded event. He studded all of ...

4. Don't TELL me we BOTH
to fuck TOM HEALEY!

5 I'm sorry but I never g...
a Blowjob during a
Kenneth Anger screening

6. You UNGRATEFUL S OB, don't accus...
me of being as unpassion...
a Robert Gober's nk!

7. I love fucking you but
hear you're a framer!

ON *SHUT UP and Love Me* I wanted to continue with the theme of sexual dysfunction that I began to write about in *The Return of the Chocolate-Smeared Woman*, but I wanted to present a female character who is not a victim and to remove rhetoric and judgment from the content. The performance starts out with me deconstructing a lap dance. Without apology,

26

SHUT UP AND LOVE ME

I admit to the audience that the performance is about sex, and about the need to connect, the need for intimacy.

Shut Up and Love Me also examines the Electra and oedipal complexes without blaming the parent. The piece is a journey into psychosexual lust and the search for meaning within the living-out of torturous personal dynamics.

In the performance, I also pour several gallons of honey onto a canvas and flip, turn and dance about naked in the golden goo. This time it isn't about violence. It is the simple pleasures of the flesh. Honey has so many meanings, but it is also just sweet.

THANKS FOR NOTHING

IT STARTED AS a waking dream. The four glasses and the teapot you gave me, crushed in the rusting Little Pony lunch box, with the words "the tortured soul of a misogynist" written inside of the lid, by me. I dreamed I gave him his lunchbox back and I woke up with a start. I decided to wait for the meaning later. I could not call my therapist, for it was Thanksgiving. A grin came to my lips and I said out loud, "He's back in town." Of course he is in town, he always came to town on Thanksgiving, to see his first set of children at his Aunt Tilly's house.

Now let us go out of the story for a moment, away from my own personality disorder, so I can get you up to speed on my take on this national holiday of bird roasting and stuffing. My six-year-old daughter puts the day into perspective. "Who cares about Thanksgiving? You don't get any presents!" Exactly. It is just a holiday where we stuff our gullets and give thanks for our health, our good fortune, our family and friends. And that is why I yearn this time of year, because I prefer to set myself up with as many losses, inadequacies, and rejections, real and imagined, as possible. I prefer to work myself into a despair, a loneliness, a wretched feeling of helplessness, of being unloved, unwanted, undesired. A desperation just short of panic—so I can relax into the sensation of sheer abandonment. A feeling without anxiety, for the anxiety takes too much energy.

Don't blame this equation on my father. He never made me feel this good.

As I told you, I woke up with a depressing feeling and I knew he was in town. It was 5:30 A.M., and I knew that if I grabbed a cab I could catch him at American Airlines, getting off the red-eye.

Being Thanksgiving, JFK was congested. I made my way into the baggage area and spotted him quickly. He was walking in his olive green corduroy jacket with matching leather trim. His hair was spiked copper. He was barrel chested. He was walking with a woman who I had named The Dog, who followed him loyally everywhere, licking his envelopes. I swear you could smell the envelope glue a mile away. I wasn't jealous, quite the contrary. She amused me, for I just wasn't the kind of woman who sets up a man's schedule to get his attention.

While I was waiting for his wits and luggage to return, I sat on the heater against the window. My tush got warmed fast. I was wearing my alpaca black full-length coat, with nothing underneath. Mostly for saving time, but also, I have a reputation to protect. After retrieving his luggage, he made a mad dash through the crowd, with The Dog licking a manila. The Dog was wearing her Sunday best, rather Thanksgiving best, and for a second I attempted a smile. I was happy for The Dog and sincerely hoped that he was regularly banging her. Just to keep the machine greased.

My ass was burning from sitting on the heater so I leaped into his path. His first reation was to act like he had just seen me yesterday. But for greater effect, he dropped his luggage and grabbed me, like a man seeing his wife after returning from war. I kissed him like a woman who is turned on to a man who would die for his country. My coat opened, with my hot naked ass available for his pleasure. I wanted to undo his belt right there, in the style of JFK, but decided to make it tantric and wait for pleasure. His hands felt my body, nude, and a thrill rushed through him, pulsing. He whispered how much he wanted me. And I felt his cock hard in our embrace. He sucked my tongue til it hurt. When he released my mouth I said just loud enough for The Dog to hear, "You'll have to shave before you eat my puss."

He slapped my rump and grabbed it for safekeeping and said, "You've always been such a goddamn hot piece of ass." I slapped him back, half teasing, half to keep up the tension, as he slid his fingers into my pelt. I looked at The Dog while my head rested on his shoulder. I faked an orgasm for her to contemplate, for I had a soft place in my heart for The Dog. I like animals.

"I'll be finished with turkey at Aunt Tilly's and the kids by nine. Meet me at the Mercer after."

The rest of the day was shot. I went home and kept the Macy's parade on while I obsessed over whether he'd show up. It was Thanksgiving so I couldn't even get my nails or hair done. After the Macy's Parade was over, I watched the Scooby Doo marathon. I obsessed if he was seeing anyone else at Tilly's, romantically, sexually. Perhaps Tilly had a new neighbor.

I wore a fishnet body stocking with an opening in the appropriate place.

The fishnet irritated my nipples and kept them at attention. Over that I wore something velvet and flimsy. Something easy to get out of.

When I got to the bar, I was early by an hour. I spotted him through the window, with a chiseled blonde who had been 27 for ten years. The blonde looked better in black than I did. For a moment I didn't go any further, in doubt about my ability to handle black nonchalantly. I made sure my Fendi bag was on my arm and walked the block.

While walking, I reassured myself that I was an adult and he was an adult and why couldn't I just relax and pretend I was in the seventies. I looked into a deli and saw the bottles of Evian and thought, because no one drinks from the goddamn tap anymore. I turned back to the Mercer Hotel.

The blonde was gone. "See, things do turn out," I said to myself. I walked up to him at the bar. He kissed my neck and held my waist as I tried to ignore her perfume. He ordered champagne. He toasted to my beauty. I wasn't listening, for I could see a blonde hair on his lapel.

We melted and giggled. Pawed and purred. We made out like teenagers who couldn't wait. He ordered the check. "I don't think we'll be wanting anything else, except each other," he said while looking at me intensely and handing the waiter his credit card.

I excused myself to pee. I made my way through the lobby of the hotel to the ladies'. I spotted the blonde coming out of the elevator. I hesitated, but only for two beats.

On my return, I saw the blonde approach him at our table. I stood emotionally frozen, incapable of doing anything, as they walked through the lobby and entered a waiting elevator. As the door closed, my heart sank to my knees. I watched the elevator go up and stop on the third floor. I waited in despair and rejection as the elevator door returned and opened empty.

He probably had her on the floor or pressed against the door, furiously fucking her.

I can't remember walking back to the table or how long I stood there, but the waiter returned his credit card and receipt to be signed. I forged his name. I put the credit card into my Fendi bag, for the next day was Black Friday, the busiest shopping day of the year.

THE AFFAIR

I COULDN'T SLEEP. I was on her side of the bed and I could see her clothes in the dry-cleaning bag under his trousers.

The issues of *Self* magazine weren't my style, nor did I care to have enough time on my hands to use her cuticle cream. I had my standards of propriety.

My husband lived one floor below and that was the main reason for the affair. It was convenient.

I know an inconvenient affair has higher stakes and is therefore more challenging, but I guess I was lazy.

I would merely say to my husband, "I'm going to mother's." And that was that, for I *was* going to mother's. This bastard was as neurotic and self-absorbed as mom. But when you are married and living one floor below, you don't want to be having an affair with someone who loves you, wants you, can't live without you. NO, that wouldn't be mom anyway. I had to get mom out of my system.

I called his wife "THE BROAD." He called her "THE SQUIRREL." She was a stewardess for Delta and her style was pure navy-and-white-with-gold-trimmings. I only saw her once in the elevator, when I had borrowed her navy blazer for the day. But THE BROAD just looked at me and said, "I have one just like it." I looked at her husband and he asked me, "What floor?"

AUTUMN FUCK

I miss New York in the fall
with an Autumn fuck
under a plaid wool skirt
that scrapes and chafes your cock
you cum on my Irish wool sweater
for Roshashanna
so I turn it inside out
sit on the street
waiting for the wife to turn up
so I can create a scene

I've learned to wait for you
with a tilt of the head
like I'm sucking on you
with my eyes slightly back

I've fucked JFK, Jr. too, Fidel and—

you want to play my daddy
you're going to have to do more
than shoot up, write bad checks
and visit my web site
or be dictator of a third world country

My father was a gambler who took me to beehives and crap rooms
stakes high, go for broke
grass never cut but smoked

If you want to play my daddy
you've got to let me drag you
out of a bar for supper
and plead with the bartender
to leave some money for jam and tea

but he had a "specialty"
He had his own special quality
you want to play my daddy
You'll have to bring a woman home
to screw while mother is in the other room.
Daddy would always say as he woke up
I have my reasons for my unconscious behavior

DOG

I saw her hair on the back of your coat. The color wasn't mine. It was long and
black and a matted mess. You were waiting for me like an old dog. Hungry and
wet
wagging that tail behind me
you old dog
Waiting by the door to be let in, fed, bathed, warmed, clothed, and dried

I don't own you but I let you follow me. Because if I didn't, this dog would be
begging and begging
barking with bow-wow bourbon breath
hoarse with collar tight
shivering with stanky dog farts
skinny naked fur
with poo matted by the tail
even flies don't come near
til I give the bone—the bone—the bone—here doggy, doggy
Looking at me with pus eyes
promising never to pee inside again
bringing me the bird at the door
can't be tamed, kept in the yard
over and under the fence
wanting to come in
to be my pet
and when doggie comes in
he wants to go out, and bites when I try to feed him
snaps when I try to to pet him

I'll never figure it out, even though I'll try with countless hours

it's something I did or didn't do—

cause you are like his mother

aren't like his mother—

What did I do?

Doesn't matter—

What didn't I do?

Doesn't matter.

IT'S PAY BACK TIME

Later when I go home—

You know what happens next—

Doggie still has the key

And doggie brings her in all jolly

I hear tongue wagging, smell your dog breath, hear your panting

as you fuck her on the bottom stair

as I listen—I've heard it before and not just with me not just with me

the porch light peeking through

shadows dancing on walls

echo of moans bouncing

I didn't get out of my bed—if you are asking—

to let the doggie out—

To ask them to stop, please

to scream, to cry

to throw them out

to watch them clutching in their desire.

I knew her

and I knew her mother well

and I made a decision

all by myself

to continue the relationship—

A DIFFERENT KIND OF INTIMACY

he'll continue the relationship with his mother, with me—
his mother who never showed him love, who tortured him
so he continues to keep hurting women the way
he was hurt, humiliated—
and I'll continue the relationship with my father, with him—
my relationship with my father which was really no relationship at all

He finished himself with her by smoking a cigarette and putting it out in my rug.
Before leaving, he looks into my darkened room and whispers—"Sweet dreams
and goodnight."
I don't know if I should see him anymore.

But the next move is mine—
The next move is mine.
The next move is all mine.

I made my first move by waiting.

I made my second move by delaying. I waited a week, then decided to stretch
it to ten days, and then made my third move. I showed up at a group of art openings at 6150 Wilshire to see a giant mirrored palm tree that rotated counter-
clockwise, huge enlarged photos of a single hair of Marilyn Monroe's, and a series
of bird droppings that caused the paper to discolor into neon, the whole mess
then laminated into placemats and shower curtains. I wore an off-white lace skirt
and I wolfed down a half-bottle of champagne. I strutted in with my titties sweat-
ing, and decided it was time to talk to the gallerist and the miserable clientele.

I laughed at what I liked, and decided to make a game out of the things I
hated by complimenting the artist and owner to the point of embarrassment.
"I have never seen a painting of ballerina slippers that look so phallicly deli-
cous—my feet are excited just looking." Mercy, I was fucking fabulous.

When he entered I didn't ignore him. I simply smiled, almost pouted, and
absent-mindedly sucked in my cheeks and licked my lips. It was my move. Well,
this threw him for a loop, for he thought he'd get some just punishment—ignor-
ing, anger, hatred, a "Hello fuckface," that man hate thang, the cold shoulder.

But no, I was ever so slightly seductive—as if I had June Singer's *Boundaries of the Soul* slipping out of my kotex pad.

We chatted about an article in the *Nation* and mid-sentence I said I was cold, and that I had left a sweater in his trunk. I took the keys. And I didn't return.

The opening was over. And there in his car, in the back seat, I was being eaten out by a 20-year-old surfer. It was dark but the street lamps gave enough of a glow and my hand was out of the window clutching the keys to his car.

My pelvis went up as I dropped the keys at his feet.

The surfer looked up and asked if he hurt me and I said, "No, you hurt him."

FIRE ISLAND

I'VE BEEN WAITING for weeks for Autumn so you can fuck me with my plaid wool skirt and pull out so the cum dribbles on my Irish-knitted sweater. I turn it inside out along the rock, against a tree, with a breeze that has been over salt and seabird's nests. Above my ass is the insignia of the brick company from 1941, you pressed so hard, and tugged my face from side to side. I washed my teeth with cider and bourbon.

We take a bus across town, and I lay myself along your lap and feel your hard cock across my face. I push my tongue along the side of your thigh and nestle my lips to the tip of your cock. I don't do anything, but the opening is there, and you want me to yourself—I lick the tip, barely, and place my hand in the space behind your balls, gently—but you like it rough, and my head is against the seat on the bus for support as you start to ram your big throbbing gristle-whip cock in my teeth—you say TAKE IT! TAKE IT! Take this big cock TAKE IT you bitch and the bus driver stares at my red hair and lips and nails to match, with cock in my mouth. He says, "That's why we live in New York City."

We need to get off—and off the bus, too—and we have a quick drink of cheap champagne, like apple juice bubble gum and ginger ale. Someone named Sly owns the place, and someone is selling quaaludes by the phone that still takes dimes. You're looking at me like I'm crazy cause you respect me, you respect my integrity, my ideals, my talents, and I say I just want you for sex. I'm waiting for you to fuck my brains out, fuck my fucking brains, fuck my fucking brains out, and you say you respect me, you respect me, but the aqua light gets in the way. He's puffing on a menthol; this place had its heyday in '79, with moustaches, lines, and leatherette. The jukebox is the same and for a minute I'm in the country, back in the small town that I never want to go to again, but I'm there at the intersection where everyone knows each other's business, where culture is knowing each other's habits, where the avant-garde is a buttered croissant, where conversation is a nonfat double latte, where citizens

believe that an investment in character comes about by buying this goddamn cheese swirl cinnamon and I do mean sin give me the sugar give the sugar pecan nuts oh, nuts between their teeth but don't worry they will floss these people floss they are a flossing people these are fear flossing people.

I loved the variety store with ric-rac and cotton hankies, with a diner that served fish on Friday in a town whose god is antiques, but instead I'm on east third street between A and B watching two men naked having sex between two parked cars, a karmann ghia and a plymouth valiant with peeling silver paint, they aren't jerking each other off they are having real faggot sex. They tell me, "Peter is fucking Paul against the hood of the ghia," and suddenly I miss my mother, suddenly I miss my mother, I miss my mother, and I'm wondering if my mother is dead yet. Are you dead yet? Are you dead yet? Are you dead yet?

Three hours after my father's funeral I was fucking in my sister's bed. I don't remember the orgasm just the fucking and I'm in a place named Sly's and all I want to do is fuck the memory away, the suffering away, the face away. I want to fuck your memory away. I look at you on the shag chair that once was a color and I put my leg on your shoulder and walk your fingers up my snake pants until you are in the snake pit—finger fuck right there in Sly's. You stop for a thirst quencher, a cheap white Russian. You tell me you aren't an intellectual and I say, "Then prove it and stop thinking and start fucking." I say, "YOU THINK TOO MUCH—I JUST WANT YOU FOR SEX— YOU THINK TOO MUCH—CAN'T YOU GET THIS THROUGH YOUR MIND—THE RELATIONSHIP HASN'T EVEN BEGUN YET—" You take another sip and look at me and I slap you before you have the chance to say you respect me.

We leave, it's only 3 A.M., and we do some poppers in a place owned by the mafia. We're hanging with a queen named Quga, so we all go to a gay bar on Fire Island, I don't know how we got there, but it was Wednesday in Chicago and then it was Saturday on Fire Island. There must have been time to sleep on the ferry. You're still wearing those Harley Davidson black shorts with your wiener hanging out—your wiener is hanging out and it's straight up on the bar stool. You're fingering me under my dress, and the queens have put a sunhat on you and taken off my heels, my panties. I left a long, long time ago and no one cares, for summer is over. It will be a long winter, with hurricanes in the air, casual detachment and emotional distancing, but all the destruction will occur with a french kiss.

DADDY

IT CAME DOWN to, you're fucking your mother, fucking your father, so why not just go for it? This is the reasoning that occured to Stella, since she had been fucking her father metaphorically all these years—why not just fucking do it literally? She had spent years in analysis working on all her fucking problems, and I do mean her fucking problems. She might as well get it over with. Her therapist actually suggested it first.

"Stella, you have been coming here for ten years, and I haven't gotten anywhere in helping you. Every man you are in love with is just an opportunity for you to relive the unresolved relationship with your father. Another adventure, to reactivate the same feelings you experienced with your father as a child. The same hurt, the same pain. And Stella, I am tired of your problem. Your problem doesn't do anything for me anymore."

So she invited her father to dinner—

He was busy. Men, she thought. She called and called him. He never returned her calls. Finally, under another pretense, she was able to see him at the office. The receptionist said he was not to be disturbed. "I'm the one who is disturbed," Stella responded.

"What is it, Stella?" he halfheartedly asked, while finishing up a call.

"Dad, let's fuck." She was browsing through a Crane's *Business Week*, and threw it down so it slid across the waxed kidney bean table, for effect.

"I've got another call, Jerry . . . "

Stella went over to her father and stroked his hair gently, and grabbed his jaw and smashed his lips together, like grandmothers do to babies. "Dad, I said I want to fuck you."

"Oh, Jerry, that's my daughter in the background—You know kids—yeah, you heard right. Wants to fuck me—probably have to take her to the Poconos or 2 Bunch Palms. You know women. For me, I can't wait—I don't need the right place. Right, Jerry, a man doesn't need the right place. Hates to hold back— when the moment, the excitement, the tension is there. Nothing stops me except making money—a deal. Yeah, tennis at six A.M.—couldn't be any earlier? Big day."

He puts down the phone.

Stella looks at him peevishly with her head tilting like she's got a case of the Katherine Hepburns.

"Dad, let's fuck, and then I can get my life going. I've been in therapy for over ten years and it's all about you. You. The way you never had any time for me. You abandoned me emotionally. Physically. And the way you treat women."

"Oh, so that's what this is about, my relationships with women."

He half chuckled while going over to the liquor cabinet and pouring himself a VO. He brought her a drink, swirled the glass and casually said, "You're not my type."

"What do you mean I'm not your type? I'm your own flesh and blood."

He swigs down the liquor hard.

"You're starting to look like your mother."

"You've never respected any of my ideas, opinions, or what I've accomplished, so why start now?" said Stella.

"I'm not saying it isn't a good idea—in theory. It's just that I'm not interested."

"You've never been interested in me. Oh, this hurts," said Stella.

"Now you're starting to sound like your mother. I'm involved with someone else. Is that easier?" He said.

"Never stopped you before. This is very important to me. Daddy, I never asked you for anything. I want you to to make love to me right here in the office."

He poured himself another one. "Dear, I don't have a condom."

"Some excuse, Dad."

"Who did you learn responsibility from, your mother?"

She refused another drink, because she wanted to make her point and not lose her train of thought. She had him cornered, listening, and it felt too good. "You're just like every other man—just concerned about number one. How about me for a change—your number-one daughter."

"Stella, you are making me feel like I have no choice. Are you asking me or telling me?"

"Oh, yeah, bring it back to you Dad, bring it back to you."

"I worked my butt off my entire life—provided you with everything money can buy."

"What I want from you money can't buy."

He's getting mad but it comes across as weariness. "You're using that Ivy League thought process I paid for on me. You think you can just come in here on my valuable time and say 'Dad, let's fuck!'? What'll it be next week? 'Let's have a three-way with Grandma. I think it would do us all a lot of good'? Or, 'Gee, I'm unhappy with my boyfriend, will you watch me go down on him and give me some pointers'? "

"Dad, you're making more of this than is necessary. All I'm asking for is a casual, one-night stand."

"I'm not a casual man."

"Do it for me."

Stella leans over the desk and brings her dress over her waist to reveal zebra panties.

"Honey, I like making the first move."

"Let me take you out of the dark ages—out of the Joey Bishop era."

"And Frank and Sammy and Dino—and I loved it, 'cause it was easy. If you're a man—you need the chase—to raise the skirt yourself—" He composes himself. Stands up. Unzips his pants to tuck in his shirt. He stares at her while straightening his tie, smoothing his hair. "Don't I pay for therapy to get rid of this nonsense?"

"Pretend I'm Ava Gardner!"

"I like Ava Gardner. Every man wanted Ava. You aren't Ava."

"It's a fantasy. Daddy, surely you've fantasized."

"Stella, this is what sluts do."

"So, I'm a fucking slut? Is that it? I'm a fucking slut? That's it—I'm not good enough for you. I've never been good enough for you. Because you don't love me. You never loved me."

A VET

SHE LOVED WARS. And Kosovo was no exception. During the Gulf War she glued herself to CNN, masturbating. It was a peculiar enactment of the idea of being "glued to the set." She would press her wet cunt to the screen, wrap her legs around the TV, and orgasm to the Gulf War jingle.

After that, she took to picking up Vietnam War vets begging for money on street corners with signs on rotting cardboard that read, "If nothing else, smile." She found that the simple straight forward approach worked the best. "Want a quarter and a beer?"

She did have her boundaries in her own unique way. And she reasoned that it was her own life and she'd do what she damned pleased.

Odd days—no beard.

Even days—beard.

She'd roll down the window of her Jetta and strain her voice over the song "War"—"Want a quarter and a beer?" It always worked. She'd bring the soldier, captain, grunt, over to her place and turn on *Apocalypse Now*, *The Deer Hunter*, *Platoon*, and watch the grunt's reaction. That was so very dear to her. Her first line of questioning would be, "So which film gets you going more, *The Deer Hunter* or *Apocalypse Now*?" And the vet would say, "When Christopher Walken puts the gun up to his head I'm a fucking goner." Usually there wasn't much sex, but plenty of beer. But still, when she had a gimp in her presence, she could never turn down the opportunity to massage the stump, lick the stump. And then pose and suggestively say to the vet "I want you to stump me." Yeah, there isn't anything like being stumped by a stump with a vet attached to it.

The vets liked her. One said to her, "I had a good time with you even though you are a civilian."

She loved to hear vets reminisce.

"I didn't want to go to war. Tried everything. Cutting off my big toe. Gaining fifty pounds. Telling them I was a queer. Should have just went to Canada.

Loved a girl there, though. Loved a beautiful Vietnamese girl. And she was blown up in my face. I loved her. Couldn't talk. But who the hell needed to talk? We just loved. Ever just love someone? Ever just love someone? There is no issue of future. No issue of communication. No issue of famiies. Just love. Pure and simple. So that is what the war taught me. Love. I see so many men. Working, Working. But not loving. A man is raised to die. A man is raised to believe that his body isn't for life, it's for death. For protecting. All cultures, the man is to be prepared to die. Give his life, if necessary."

Because the dynamics were fatherly, familiar, you'd think she'd call them daddy. No—she called them pappy.

It was never anything that was planned or calculated, like a specific fetish or S&M session. It was just a way for her to feel a man's pain, the pain of being raised to die. That's it—that was the turn on for her—that men, boys, are essentially raised to be worthless. Their lives are nothing—meaningless. They can, will, die for their country, their family, their wife, their children, their flag. They walk around like they own the goddamn world—but any day the draft, the war— Every day, another man makes a war with other men, and a mother gives birth to another soldier to save her—to protect her—to die for her, for the country, for god.

This was the intention, the truth behind her act, her fascination—and it turned her on to no end. For here, she felt all-powerful, where her femaleness had some goddamn commonsense. And that she was with men who would die for her. She was with a man who would die for her. She was worth dying for.

DELICATE BOY

THE BOY, DELICATE and good and fair, blue-eyed and laughing and sensitive. His mother stopped touching him when he was two. For she had hit him. He did something that children will do. But her hand went out of control and she had hit him, in a way that she woke up and went to sleep with, and after that she never held her son. The boy was never held, never touched, never cuddled, never stroked, never smoothed, never cooed too, never kissed, never shown love.

When I see you, there are moments I want to be your mother and hold your head on my lap and stroke your hair while the moon rises, and it is a full moon, and I will rub the small of your back and hold your feet like little cookies and take little bites of toes. I'll roll you into a ball and hold you on my belly and rub and smooth your shoulders, and I'll kiss your forehead and tell you you are the sweetest boy, the loveliest boy, there is no other boy like you, no other boy I love as much as you. I will rock you in my arms and coo in your ears and make the monsters go away, the creepies go away to places far away, and you're safe in my arms, and my bosom breathes deeply, and you may cry if you like. I hold you, my child. I hold you til morning light and kiss your cheek, for it is day now and my boy has woken and I wash his face and behind his ears and bathe him gently with softening scents that loosen the sand in ears, and I wash his hair and massage his scalp and I wait for him to make his pee while I gather up the big bath towel that is bigger than he is, and I dry my boy down and I tickle him. We fall to the floor laughing, giggling. I love my boy. I love my boy. I love my boy.

When he was five his kindergarten teacher wore silk stockings and he sat next to her as she read and with his boy hand he felt her legs. The legs felt so smooth and soft and he kept his hand on her leg and slowly moved up her leg. He had small hands and he loved to touch soft things, because he was never touched at home. He loved his kitty. He loved his blankie. This was the first time he had been away from his mother, and sitting next to the the soft legs, stroking the legs, was like holding a wild animal, it was like holding himself, because it was he who needed to be held. The reading and the softness of her voice. The timing, the rhythm like a heartbeat, a breath, and he wanted to touch and be touched so much.

The teacher didn't pull away, but allowed the boy to hold and stroke her leg. Later, she called the boy's parents and told them that there was something wrong with their son. No longer was there anything wrong with the mother, but now there was something wrong with the boy.

From then on the boy desired legs. He was so fascinated, so curious about them.

Whenever I see you I always wear stockings with garters and seams, French hosiery with velvet cutouts of lacy patterns, black teasers with seams that go up my ass with garters and white lacy frills, shoes black and pointy and heels that dig and penetrate and make my long legs longer.

I let you fuck me standing up under a peach tree against a brick wall in the courtyard of an Irish tavern, next to a church called St. Dymphna. And I can feel you for a week and then you are gone.

DONA ANN McADAMS

DAVID WOJNAROWICZ and Karen Finley are shooting the breeze, and catching a few far from the innocent culprits of right-wing America's forces of oppression in the cross-fire. Sitting in on this dialogue rates as one of the most memorable and historic moments I've ever had as a writer. Wojnarowicz and Finley are not only

27

TONGUES OF FLAME

prominent figures, among the most exceptional, talented and outspoken voices of our age, but they have distinguished themselves as ferociously indominable artists and advocates of society's abused and disaffected minorities. At a time when an ugly slew of ideologically monomaniacal headhunters have positioned themselves as a self-righteous thought police aggressively monitoring an absurd, fascistic moral imperative in the arts, these two artists have refused to back away from the insulting slanderous character assassinations, antagonistic intolerances and unconstitutional acts of suppression being launched against them, and instead have chosen to fight back through the courts and through their own artistic gestures. As media headlines and moral majority marginalization have sensationalized their work, it is important for all of us to step back and seriously consider the artistic merit, moral integrity, social accuracy and political correctness of their unflinching expression. This interview is an attempt to address the discrepancy between the truth of their actions and the misrepresentations and harassments that plague them.

—CARLO MCCORMICK,
Paper, October 1990

DW: Do you know that Ollie North has been fund raising for Helms using your work and mine?

KF: Well great, because aren't we using him in our work?

DW: He sent out this letter saying "Dear Freedom Partner," and dished your work and mine and a handful of gay activists. The thing that made me laugh is that he was picked up about 20 years ago running around naked in the suburbs of Virginia with a handgun.

KF: You know how you were saying how Wildmon was really like an artist in his appropriation of your work. It would be really great to get all these people and the stuff that they're making and have a show of it. Did you guys hear about the Jesse Helms portrait contest they're having in North Carolina? One of his people is actually going to be a judge.

DW: I did a portrait of him. I have this show coming up in November called "In the Garden," so I did a color photograph of this garden with lush beautiful flowers, and on a leaf is an ugly looking spider with a swastika on its abdomen, and a little head of Jesse Helms. On the back it says "Subspecies: Helms Senatorius. This arachnid is found in Washington, D.C. and North Carolina and is responsible for cutting safe sex education for lesbians and gays." Maybe I should send it in.

DW: Just to underline their tactics—how they form images and information.

CM: I know you're both going through the same sort of bullshit, and I understand you two talk with each other about it every now and then.

KF: We saw each other at the trial. When there's legal situations going on, or when you're having your work taken out of context, it's very difficult for people to understand how it eats you up inside. You get so angry from it. Your life gets focused on it. You want to get even. You want to have your name cleared. I feel that David understands that.

DW: Or about how Wildmon looks like Baby Huey with a cowlick.

KF: David, do you remember during the trial you said that you were going to do some drawings of him. Do you think you are?

DW: Yeah, I've done a few drawings of Wildmon of the deposition that he had to give to my lawyers. They were drawings of him at a pig fest, getting petunias put in his behind and stuff like that. One of my lawyers asked him if he ever won an award. He got really golly-gee bashful about it and said 'Gosh, if you insist upon knowing, Larry Flint named me asshole of the month.' My lawyer said she didn't think that qualified as an award and then had to refresh his memory about Ad Week magazine giving him a marketer of the year award.

KF: I liked it when he was asked if he knew what a collage was.

DW: His lawyer asked him, "Mr. Wildmon, do you know the difference between a portrait and a collage?" and he goes "No, ahh don't." Karen, do you have any idea when the trial is going to come up for the law suit you brought against the NEA?

KF: We filed September 27th, and I don't know how long it's going to take. I'm sure there's going to be the depositions. You've been through that.

DW: Yeah, I did a six- or seven-hour deposition with Wildmon's lawyers.

KF: Did you get to have your lawyers present?

DW: Absolutely. But the weird thing about depositions is that you have to answer everything regardless if the lawyers object. So they were asking me really creepy stuff like what I thought about Mapplethorpe's "sexually provocative child photos." I asked them to describe these pictures and they said "unclothed or partially clothed children." Then I told them that the only place I had ever seen them was on *The 700 Club*, and when I looked at them I had no sexual feelings at all, so I can only imagine that Pat Robertson did. Anyway, they weren't so happy about the deposition.

KF: Okay, I'll be ready. Have you gotten the dollar that you were awarded in the law suit yet?

DW: No, actually I'm going to get it pretty soon. I'm really excited. I'm going to use it to buy an ice cream cone or a condom, depending on how hot I feel.

KF: Is it going to be a check or what?

DW: It's going to be a check signed by old Baby Huey himself.

KF: Oh my goodness, aren't you going to keep it?

DW: I think I'm going to enlarge it to something like 16 by 20 feet and do a piece on it. Maybe I'll cover myself with paint and fuck it.

KF: I think you should have the handwriting analyzed, especially the "One Dollar," to find out about the loop. Fronhmayer is coming here to Chicago in a few days. Did you hear about Tim Miller, who is one of the artists whose grant got denied. He was doing a performance in Atlanta, and Lynn Schutte, who runs a performance space in San Diego, was up there and happened to run into Fronhmayer in a bar there and got him to go to Tim's show.

CM: In a way that's good, because when these people are asked if they've actually seen the work they're condemning, the common response is something like— "no, I wouldn't look at that."

DW: But Fronhmayer is pretty brain dead as it is. I think even if he witnessed the performance it wouldn't make any difference.

KF: Don't you think that he's really smart and knows exactly what he's doing?

DW: No I'm pretty repulsed by his actions. They should have fired his ass a long time ago. Is it smart that on the backs of a handful of people he manipulated his position within the NEA and set up a system where he's going to judge artistic merit, when he obviously doesn't know beans about the creative act or expression? Bottom line, his remark that 'you wouldn't want to hang a picture of the Holocaust in the front room of a museum,' should have gotten him fired. He's totally grotesque.

CM: I think the scary thing about what is happening is not so much any real fear I may have about you two being censored out of existence, because I think they'd need a firing squad to silence you, but it's more about this sort of self-censorship on all levels that this harassment is breeding.

KF: Our careers are escalating, of course careers do, but I don't know about you David, I'm noticing places and situations where I'm not performing at. There still are a lot of places that are very scared to put me on. Also, there are a lot of small performance spaces that are receiving these letters inquiring if they have any intention of having me perform there. So, there is this fear before a place even puts me on that there is going to be trouble, that their funding could get taken away, that their files could be impounded, that they really could be under a tremendous amount of scrutiny just for presenting me. And I think that some of these spaces, given that type of possible harassment, aren't going to be presenting me.

DW: Yeah, and you get up into the hierarchy of the art world. These one page ads decrying censorship put out by museums and other institutions are a bunch of bullshit. These people haven't put their names/faces/money on the line at all. Their curatorial efforts have always excluded people like us. It's just the rare bone that comes sailing through once in a while. If they had any guts at all, or any blood in their bodies, they'd be putting themselves on the line in a real way. What the hell is culture? It's certainly not somebody's blue-chip collection.

KF: What I'm really excited about is trying to get artists to be organized, to get artists to become political. I think what's happened for hundreds of years is this idea that the artist is crazy. That's the whole reason for the Van Gogh phenomenon. Everyone loves Van Gogh more for his being out of his mind and out of control, which is what they want to believe creativity is, than for his paintings. No one could think that a person who is intelligent, or is a professional, or who thinks, could create work. The idea is that creativity only comes out of irrationality.

DW: What's hilarious is that they've picked on performance artists, who are probably some of the most articulate people, because they not only work with sound or verbal techniques, but they use images and gestures. So they've executed every possible gesture or expression that the human body can make, and they're very articulate. They definitely picked on the wrong people. Wildmon is creating this crack legal team to go out and create nuisance suits against artists that they find reprehensible. So there are probably going to be a lot more trials on the local and state level.

CM: The general perception of how this excess of media attention has effected you both is that you're each happily swimming in gravy now. The most common comment I hear has to do only with how great this has been for your careers. One thing I think people fail to recognize is how, as you mentioned Karen, this has created such an emotional stress in your lives.

KF: Yes, I feel that it devours your ability to actually create, first of all with the time that is involved in trying to defend yourself. People aren't interested so much in the work, but in the sound bite of controversy. There is so much energy involved, because I feel a responsibility to defend the arts, so that with the interviews I'm forced to do all this clarifying and to be on top of everything. With the legal case, I have to try to really be up on everything that's happening politically. That takes a tremendous amount of time. There is also this sense of self-censorship in terms of knowing what you're going to create and how it's going to be looked at. I think as much as David and I are making jokes and laughing about it here, there's still the situation that you think, oh wow, when you go and write this it's going to be looked at in this different light—it's either blasphemy or sacrilegious or obscene. So you're carrying that, and now I always have that thought process when I'm creating work. That just always affects you.

DW: Yeah, it's like creating stuff in a public context instead of a private context. The dialogue that one has with oneself for years, it's as if you're taking a bath and you're surrounded by 300 people waiting to see which way the water falls. It's very wearing. Tell me there's nothing to the assassination of spirit, which is what the gestures of Rohrbacher and Helms and Dannemeyer and North and Wildmon are all about. Their attempt is to shut down a flow of information and assassinate the spirit. To have a best seller or a sold-out show or performance doesn't deal with the psychic weight of that kind of assassination. I remember looking at a *New York Post* editorial about me that said I was somebody who would worship Hitler. Do people understand what the weight of that is? Or to have somebody on the *700 Club* suggest that my work might be part of a satanic plot to undermine the fabric of America. They throw out these red flags that are really designed to kill the spirit.

CM: The oppression of personal spirit you both speak of could well be the intention of this right wing thought police, but one effect of this battle they have not anticipated, I think, is the radicalization of a number of people who may have had radical views, but who were not necessarily radical activists per se. I've noticed this in both of your cases, how you've been backed into a corner where you've essentially been forced into a much more aggressive, public, and antagonistic mode, and a much more intensely activist agenda.

KF: I feel that our freedom, or ability to create is being threatened and has become the number one priority for me. We were talking before about museums and art institutions emphasizing art as decoration, or art just in terms of the history of aesthetics. What has happened is that art's political responsibility or responsibility to humanity has been ignored. How do you think the establishment, the big deal galleries and collectors, are responding to this? Do you think they're involved enough?

DW: No, because these are the people who really need to be held accountable—the people on the boards, the collectors, the people that own the institutions with the secret weight of money. Those are the people who are least involved at this point; they've reduced art to a non-functional object and continue to create a market for it because they don't give a shit about it. They don't care about suppression of information, identity, or anything else, and they've always been involved in that. There are a handful of people in institutions who have put their jobs, their bodies, their names on the line, but not the majority of people who can make a difference because of the weight of their bank accounts.

DW: What kind of America do you think people like Wildmon, Rohrbacher and Helms would be satisfied with?

KF: The image that came in my mind—do you remember Captain Kangaroo? Where they had that opening with this little train and this artificial miniature town, sort of like *Mr. Rogers' Neighborhood*, and there's this hand moving trucks? That's what I see. And there's no people there. I see a country where there are no people.

DW: I remember these movies I used to go see for 15 cents out at the local firehouse in New Jersey when I was a kid. There were these zombie films made in the '40s where everybody walked around with popping eyeballs after drinking some kind of lotus potion. That's the kind of America I see—pure zombie society.

KF: I think we should do a story called *The Holy Family*.

DW: We could do a biblical scene; we could modernize the bible. I mean here's a book where they quote some guy from a time when they didn't have tape recorders, we might as well bring it up to date.

KF: I hope I get a chance to play Jesus.

DW: Well, we could do a siamese twin Jesus, with your head and my head, wearing diapers. The wisemen can bring us yams and diapers.

DW: It's the only kind of art we can make since we're under a Christian occupation in this country.

&DITOR'S NOTE: When Barney Rosset was in grade school, he and a friend started a journal called *The Sommunist*. The name derived from a combination of "socialist" and "communist." Later, they abandoned the name in favor of the classically punk Anti-Everything.

28

BORN TO
RAISE HELL

What's remarkable is that this took place in the 1930s, forty years before punk was invented.

Barney Rosset's sensibility has always been as prescient as it is subversive. Rosset was the publisher of Grove Press in the 1950s and 1960s, and in that capacity he brought out many "underground" classics, including the works of Samuel Beckett, Henry Miller, and William S. Burroughs. He fought numerous legal battles over his right to publish such books, and the public's right to read them, and won landmark decisions in the *Lady Chatterly's Lover*, *Naked Lunch* and *Tropic of Cancer* trials.

In part, this book is a history of the culture wars of the 1980s and 1990s. These "wars" are of course part of an ongoing cultural dynamic that encompasses the uproar over the "Sensation" exhibit at the Brooklyn Museum of Art, and extends back in time to the McCarthy hearings and beyond. It seemed important to add a historical dimension to the account of the trial of the "NEA 4." And there seemed to be no better way of doing this than to get the perspective of Barney Rosset, who has been in the trenches for over fifty years. Barney Rosset and Karen Finley met for a discussion, which I facilitated, in New York on June 26, 2000.

—Elizabeth Schambelan

KF: I wanted to know, Barney, when you became known as the publisher of scandalous books, and the distributor of movies like *I Am Curious, Yellow*—what was it like being in the eye of the storm, scrutinized by the public as a troublemaker? Like, "Barney Rosset, what's he doing now?"

BR: It aggravated the hell out of me, that attitude—"What is it now?" Then on the other hand I'd think, "Well, if they want something, I'll give it to them." For example, with *I Am Curious, Yellow*—I thought of it as a very urgent plea for women's rights. And it's a very good film—not the greatest in history, but good. But I knew that it was going to get this reaction. By then I had gone through enough of that sort of thing, and I saw something that was good on its own merits but which some people would object to violently. So that was a temptation.

With *I Am Curious, Yellow*, we ultimately lost before the Supreme Court, but by then nobody noticed. The court voted four to four, which meant that we lost. One of the justices, William O. Douglas, wouldn't vote. His excuse was that we had published an excerpt from his autobiography in the *Evergreen Review*. I think that was just an excuse, though, because he was under severe political attack at the time. He was very closely associated with a foundation from Chicago, which had some dubious antecedents. He was the head of it, and Gerald Ford was attacking him. At the same time, we were attacking Nixon in the *Evergreen Review*. We had a nude photograph next to a photograph of Nixon, and Ford waved it around in Congress. Ford was really after Douglas. And so Douglas declared himself out. It saddened me that he didn't have enough guts to do what he knew was right.

KF: How many cases did you have that went to the Supreme Court?

BR: Two or three. For me, personally, the whole censorship thing climaxed emotionally in Chicago. A *Tropic of Cancer* trial was held there (There were literally dozens of others). When we were brought to trial there, everybody said, "Oh, you're gonna lose here, that's for dead certain." It was the only case in which I was ever a witness. The district attorney was supremely confident. He said, "You don't really care about this book: you're only publishing it because you want to make money off of it." But I had a paper I had written on the book, at Swarthmore, years before in 1940 or 1941. I took it out and I started reading this paper, which attempted to show how important as a work of art this book was. The district attorney tried to shut me up, but the point was made.

So we won, and that judge was criticized 'til the day he died for deciding in our favor, but he did. It was a historic decision, one applauded by a huge segment of the literary editors, critics and publishers of this country. I thought *Tropic of Cancer* was a great book, and I got caught up in this maelstrom deliberately. There was no other way of going forward. I just didn't know how to turn around. I was a long distance runner; I was on the cross-country running team in college. That's the only thing I did at Swarthmore that I liked, and the only person who asked me to come back for a second year, after I dropped out, was the track coach. Cross-country runners don't quit.

KF: I want to know, what was it like for the authors who were going through these court battles?

BR: Well, Henry Miller was not involved at all. He remained outside for the most part. We did publish an impassioned and beautiful plea "Defense of the Freedom to Read," which he wrote for the Supreme Court of Norway. It was on behalf of this book SEXUS, we printed it in *Evergreen Review* No. 9 in 1959.

KF: What about *Naked Lunch*, Burroughs?

BR: Oh, Burroughs was fine. He was cool, just cool. But he wasn't very involved either on a day-to-day basis. For these writers, their message was contained within their works.

ES: Norman Mailer wasn't a Grove author, but he took sort of an activist role, didn't he? He was a witness in the *Naked Lunch* trial.

BR: Yes; he was fantastic. The judge attacked him, but he was very good. We also went to court over a great documentary film, *Titicut Follies*, and Norman was a witness there, too. The film was a study of a prison for the criminally insane in Massachusetts. I think it's a masterpiece, done by the director, Frederick Wiseman. Anyway, we were distributing it, and immediately got arrested in Massachusetts. The warden of the prison had begged Wiseman to make the film, to show what a lousy place the prison was so he could get some additional funds in order to improve conditions, and Wiseman made it. And then it was banned in Massachusetts, supposedly because of sexual implications involving aged men. So we had a big trial in Boston. In the movie, an old man is playing a saxophone and masturbating – that was why it was too sexy, this old, old man – and at the trial the judge said, "Do you think that's all right, him doing that, playing the saxophone and masturbating?" And Norman said, "Yes."

KF: Norman displays a strong persona that handles the attacks of censorship- even if that means being a soldier for other authors. We know about the political problems of censorship but there is also the personal cost, the psychic cost to the soul when the artist has to be constantly defending his work like we saw with Lenny Bruce, who in the end, only spoke of his troubles, his work was about his trials.

But for me, fighting had less to do with "my" art and more to do with the larger principles of free speech. I was always a political person, though. I think, coming from Chicago, I always felt like I had to have a political position.

BR: I was also always political; I never thought about it that way, though. I grew up in Chicago, like you, Karen, but earlier than you, during the Depression. My first hero was John Dillinger. I thought he was, well, Robin Hood. In seventh grade, I remember getting a petition out to all the other students to give to the government, saying, "Stop it! Leave this man alone. We need people like this." The eighth grade was the biggest year of my life. We had a wonderful teacher, Sarah Greenabaum — Parker has maintained a foundation in her name to this day. We studied the history of China in remarkable depth, and on one of the very first tests, she asked about the Sung Dynasty. What was the situation for women during the Sung Dynasty? What did binding feet do to them economically, and what kind of people thought of doing that? And I, on the test, interjected out of nowhere, "The American government is corrupt!" I don't know if she gave me a point for that or not — but she didn't subtract anything. She was a strong influence on me.

Then I went to Swarthmore, and while I was there somebody — a very bright guy who later became curator of prints at the Met — said, "You ought to read a book called *Tropic of Cancer*." That was in 1940.

KF: How old were you?

BR: Eighteen. So I went into Gertrude Steloff's Gotham Book Mart in New York, at his instructions, and bought a copy of *Tropic of Cancer*. And I read it, I wrote a paper on it, and then I quit school for a few weeks. In the paper, I denounced the miserable cultural situation in the United States following Miller's lead. That, to me, was the lesson of *Tropic of Cancer*. I barely noticed the sex. I just loved his attacks on America. I said, "Who could read a book like this and stay in this place?" The professor gave me a B minus, saying, "Perhaps the jaundice was in the eyes of the beholders," presumably meaning Miller and myself. So I literally ran away. I wanted to escape to Mexico, but ended up in Miami, and when my money ran out, I had to creep back in shame to Swarthmore. But I liked that book. I mean I *really* liked it. And when I finally got involved in publishing, a lot of it hinged on my desire to eventually publish *Tropic of Cancer*. And so that stayed my objective until I actually achieved it in 1962.

KF: Well, who was publishing it at that time?

BR: Olympia Press, headed by Maurice Girodias in Paris. His father, Jack Kahane had brought it out through his Obelisk Press in 1937 in English and Maurice went on with it after the war. He was instrumental in getting Henry Miller to agree to let me publish it. As I became more sophisticated, I decided that it would be better to try *Lady Chatterly* first, utilizing Lawrence's reputation as a great writer. So that was a form of deliberate provocation, but also a carefully thought out way to create a survivable environment for *Tropic of Cancer*—with *Lady Chatterly's* Lover. But it took about fifteen years more to get *Tropic of Cancer* out in the United States.

ES: You didn't really know much about publishing before you started, right?

BR: Very, very little. Most directly my efforts came about through the painter Joan Mitchell, who had gone to Parker four years behind me and to whom I was later married. After WWII she studied at the Art Institute in Chicago. Oddly, one of the very important people there, a supporter of Joan's work was Katherine Kuh who was related to my eighth grade teacher, Sarah Greenabaum. Joan got her Masters degree there and she won a traveling fellowship. We went and lived in Paris. Most Americans there then were on the GI Bill. It was quite an exciting moment. I didn't know any writers of note. I was much closer to painters than to writers – painters are more gregarious. They seemed to enjoy themselves much more than writers. Writers tend to get hidden away in some closet. We got married there, and we came back, and settled in New York. In the meantime, I had produced a feature film *Strange Victory*. It depicted, in a very bitter way, the depth of racial discrimination in post war America. And after, I attended the New School on the GI Bill. Gradually, and sadly for me, Joan began drifting away. I mean, she moved a block away. That's a meaningful sign – when your wife moves away a block away. "Don't worry, I'll be back . . ." I waited one year. "When are you coming back?" "Oh, soon."

Of course, she didn't come back. But she remained a strong supporter and she sent over an old friend with some books, an armful of orphaned books. Joan had gone to the Art Institute with this friend, Franeine Felsenthal who she said knew these two guys who'd published three books, under the name Grove Press, named after the street in the West Village. They were Melville's *The Confidence Man, The Writings of Aphra Behn*, and the poetry of Richard Crashaw. They had published these books, then ran out of funds, an occurrence which I found to be quite common in the publishing profession. Would that be something for me to get involved in? I thought, "That's interesting, why not?" So I got the books, literally — but I didn't know what to do with them and they were filling up my apartment. So I went to Columbia and took a course in publishing. After I bought the company, Grove Press, I met Don Allen, who had been a naval officer in the Japanese Intelligence section. He was extraordinarily bright. He eventually became my co-editor of *Evergreen Review*, which started in 1957 and we stayed on Ninth Street and took an additional apartment in the brownstone next door. We took the books to the post office in a grocery cart for a number of years.

KF: I was wondering what your feelings are about publishing now, or in recent years, in terms of the problems people have been having with the Christian right, the Christian Coalition – bookstores being sued over the sales of photography books, Jock Sturges, Sally Mann. . . . And it's happening with comic books and other genres. What do you think about the current climate in publishing and bookselling?

BR: I think it is much better than it was fifteen years ago. In 1985 I was more or less put out of business by the Christian Coalition. Some reverend down South threatened to boycott Kmart because of my books, and Kmart told Walden, its bookstore chain at the time, to stop selling them. And Barnes & Noble followed suit. So we were hurt badly. It was a bad situation. However, to the credit of Barnes & Noble, one day, the president, Leonard Riggio, whom I had never met, called me on the phone. He said, "Come on over and see me," and I did, and he put his arms around me, said he had changed his mind and they took back our books. That helped a lot.

KF: So are you saying that you think that wouldn't have happened earlier, before 1985? That it was because of those big conglomerates, Kmart and Barnes & Noble, that it happened?

BR: I don't know. In book publishing now, just as in the rest of life, some people are getting richer and richer, and the rest of the people, who you don't hear too much about, are not getting richer and richer. So in book publishing, yes, the "conglomerates" have achieved tremendous power, but on the other hand, there are more small book publishers, today, than ever at any time since I've been involved in the book world. So in that sense there's kind of a flowering, in small publishing. On the other hand the companies that were great, the big ones, like Random House, Simon & Schuster, Scribners, and Doubleday, that were great book publishing companies then – are today, as far as I can see, more and more submerged in giant "multimedia" conglomerates.

ES: It's interesting to me that you said that your wife went to Europe on a fellowship, and that a lot of people in Paris were on the GI bill. So you're saying that the expatriate climate in Paris at that time was made possible by public funding.

BR: That's true.

ES: The *NEA 4* lawsuit was concerned with the idea of the government funding art, and what the boundaries of its rights and responsibilities should be when it does that. How do you feel about that—the idea of government funding artists or artistic expression? And do you think that withholding that funding is a form of censorship?

BR: I certainly think withholding it is a form of censorship. But it's been that way throughout the history of art – rich families or governments giving money to artists, as long as they like what the artists are doing, and when they don't like it, they withdraw it.

KF: Even in situations where there's no public funding, there is still censorship. Society will find some way to censor what it doesn't want to hear. With Guilianni here in New York, you'll get laws about nightclubs—It'll go into fun, it'll go into lifestyle—I think I was naïve about that in the beginning. I felt that I had to make a statement about what was happening in the arts, or in America—that we needed to hear different voices, hearing people who were gay, women, people of color. I think that's what it was about, and I think that's also what the GI Bill did. It mostly benefited men, but it brought opportunities to people who wouldn't necessarily have had those opportunities otherwise. For me, suing the government had to do with the fact that we felt it was unconstitutional to deny funding because of a vague restriction called "decency." That vagueness is an opportunity, a device by the government to restrict speech that it considers offensive.

BR: I agree

KF: Art History occupies a dialogue within itself. Impressionism reacted against hyper-realism and the invention of photography – or punk in reaction to the peace, love hippie culture. Ethnic art-making, women's art, queer culture all first respond in reaction to the dominant culture that they feel left out of. Gradually, we see this disappear as the power equalizes.

BR: But in actually doing your work, you got an organic part of yourself into trouble. It wasn't just defending other people. It's one thing to say, "OK, I don't care, you've got a right to say what you want to say and I'll fight for your right to say it," and another thing to be the one saying it, creating it. I mean that's a lot tougher. And a lot more important.

KF: But I never really expected to get myself in trouble, it just seemed like I kept on getting in trouble.

BR: On stage, there are so many things that could aggravate and pro-voke different people—the way you look, the way you speak, your movements towards other people. All of these things could be very wonderful to some and really infuriating to others. There's a guy who murdered a number of nurses in Chicago, Richard Speck—we published a book about him. It's called *Born to Raise Hell*. I think that hell-raising is not something you do on purpose. You just can't stop yourself. And then, of course, there are the consequences. There are set guidelines, good or bad, for dealing with murderers. The latter is applicable to artists like you, Karen. Your very being, your creative core car-ries you outside of our current cultural clichés. This can be and is very upsetting to us. The heart of the matter for us, the audi-ences, the publishers, the art entrepreneurs, the politicians, is ultimately how we as a people deal with those rare individuals exemplified by you. This is our challenge. Do we provide clear waters for you in which to swim, to explore our humanness in its infinite facets or do we dam you up in a cul de sac of petty obstacles and false problems, keeping you and ourselves from the verification of life as something expanding and exhilarating? You are here to give us the kind of organic explosion, which only people like you can give. If we hinder you, stop you in any way, then we do so at our own peril.

FOR NEIL

THE LIGHTS ARE out, but we make our way with touch, something velvet and maroon, like bedroom slippers. I take your arm and glide your skin against my thigh. I light the candle of lemon magnolia, and we pass the cedar closet where the towels are kept. Outside is a lake. Our eyes are used to the darkness and a faint new moon, we only met yesterday and still managed to get here. We find the bathroom, it is a room with only a tub, and the hot water still works. You are behind me and you hold my gingham skirt. I left my white cotton panties at the beach. I turn on the water and let the rust wash out and make the water as hot as possible. I pull your linen shirt off of you and your pants down and I run my hands across your chest. In a bottle are sage green salts and I put them in the water. In my skirt are petals of summer roses and orange peel, which I add to your bath. I help you into the water and let you sit and I get on my knees and use the lavendar soap. I lather and massage your back and skin. I make a lather and wash your thighs and feet and toes and neck and fingers. I come down to your cock and I massage and let it grow. I keep doing it as I kiss you all wet, as you lay back, and I have your balls in my other hand, holding tight and firm, and the smoothness of your skin—I want to eat you. I push firmly on your cock so it is straight up against your firm belly. I need to touch you now like no other time and I hold the top of your cock and move fast and then slow, so very slow, so very slow, I keep doing it, for you don't want me to stop, and I never will.